T0300794

# ADVANCE PRAISE

*"Magnus's book shares the good, the bad and the ugly of becoming a global keynote speaker. Raw, honest, valuable – and often very funny – advice that I wished I had read before I started my global speaking career."*

**FREDRIK HAREN**
The Creativity Explorer (spoken in 75 countries on six continents)

*"This is an astoundingly generous book, written by a likewise generous professional. I have more than a thousand gigs in 33 countries under my belt. I had no idea I had this much yet to learn."*

**ANDREAS EKSTRÖM**
Author, reporter and speaker on all things digital, working with and for partners all around the world

*"Witnessing Magnus speak in 2010 was a revelation – it wasn't just a presentation, it was a performance. Magnus didn't just speak; he commanded the stage and captivated his audience. This book captures that electrifying experience and will ignite your passion to become a professional global speaker. Let Magnus inspire you, just as he inspired me!"*

**NANCY RADEMAKER**
Global speaker on technology and trends

*"I'm blown away! Having done over 1,000 paid speaking gigs worldwide, I thought I knew everything. But this book has transformed me, making me feel like a newborn. A must-read for anyone looking to elevate their speaking career."*

**STEFAN HYTTFORS**
Author of *Yoga for Leaders* and
two-time winner of Speaker of The Year

Published by
**LID Publishing**
An imprint of LID Business Media Ltd.
LABS House, 15-19 Bloomsbury Way,
London, WC1A 2TH, UK

info@lidpublishing.com
www.lidpublishing.com

A member of:

**BPR** ⊛
businesspublishersroundtable.com

All rights reserved. Without limiting the rights under copyright
reserved, no part of this publication may be reproduced, stored or
introduced into a retrieval system, or transmitted, in any form or
by any means (electronic, mechanical, photocopying, recording
or otherwise) without the prior written permission of both the
copyright owners and the publisher of this book.

© Magnus Lindkvist, 2024
© LID Business Media Limited, 2024

Printed by Imak Ofset
ISBN: 978-1-915951-57-1
ISBN: 978-1-915951-58-8 (ebook)

Cover and page design: Caroline Li

MAGNUS LINDKVIST

# THE BUSINESS OF
# SPEAKING

## THE 10 COMMANDMENTS
## TO BECOMING A
## SUCCESSFUL SPEAKER

MADRID | MEXICO CITY | LONDON
BUENOS AIRES | BOGOTA | SHANGHAI

To Karoline, who has kept me
in the speaking business for longer
than I could have ever imagined.

# CONTENTS

AN OPENING

# THE BEST SPEECH I'VE EVER GIVEN

The taxi was late.

Or, rather, I was late getting into the taxi.

When I asked how long the journey to the airport would take, the driver politely replied, "With some luck, we will be there by midnight."

That was half an hour after my flight was to depart.

I would have to Plan B this thing.

I rebooked the flight for the following morning and texted the client, profusely apologizing and blaming the late taxi.

Using up karma.

I don't believe in fuzzy concepts like karma and cosmic justice.

An American or German client would never have agreed to last-minute schedule changes without putting up a good fight.

This client merely replied, "OK! We moved your session to after lunch."

Although I don't believe in fuzzy concepts like karma and cosmic justice, this client scored a big win in the great beyond.

*Man, am I going to deliver a knockout speech tomorrow,* I thought to myself as I drifted off to sleep at a shabby airport hotel.

When I landed the next morning, it was a crystal clear, cold winter day. The sun was shining, and the snowy fields around the long, straight roads from the airport to the city glittered like silver. It was going to be a good day, I felt.

At the colossal ice hockey arena the client had rented for the event, hundreds – nay, thousands – of people were having boxed lunches. I was to be the first speaker after lunch. A sales company celebrating its 20th anniversary of doing business, the audience consisted of sales reps from around the country. In my experience, sales and HR are the two best groups to speak in front of, as they tend to be outgoing, rowdy and eager to understand new ideas quickly. If you're curious, chief financial officers are the complete opposite.

I made my way into the arena, where a circular stage with giant screens perched above it had been built. It looked more like a rock show than a corporate event. Having once had rock-star dreams crushed by a general lack of musical talent, I felt a tingle ... a bundle of nerves vibrating inside me. I was thrilled and even a little bit nervous. I had done hundreds of corporate speeches over the past decade, but nothing like this.

"What a great day," I whispered to myself.

At that moment, the guys behind the mixing desk – phenomenally important to be on good terms with for any speaker – asked if I had brought my presentation.

"Ehhh ..." I stuttered, "I sent it to you a few weeks ago."

They all shook their heads.

Well, never mind, I shrugged and opened my laptop to transfer a copy of my presentation to them.

The Wi-Fi was slow.

It was so slow that, for the first time in a long time, I was able to see the old, famous Microsoft icon, where sheets of paper are transferred from one folder to another with a countdown bar and time below. It would take more than 40 minutes to transfer the presentation.

My speaking slot was due to begin in less than 20 minutes.

As I was thinking about how to speed up the transfer, a well-dressed man approached me.

"Hello, Magnus, I am Dmitry, your translator," he said in a thick Eastern European accent.

Translators are another group of people whom you must be on good footing with. For parts of the audience, the translator – not me – delivers the spoken part of a speech.

"Hello, Dmitry." I smiled and complimented him on the impeccable suit and tie.

And I asked why he was wearing a head mic.

Normally, translators are squeezed into a small glass cage at the back of the room, with a jug of water at room temperature and a microphone. The audience members wear headphones where the translated words will flow forth.

"I will be with you onstage," he said matter-of-factly, and it slowly dawned on me that this would change every part of my speech.

"You mean, the translation is consecutive?" I asked while trying to smile and conceal the sinking feeling inside me.

"Yes," Dmitry replied enthusiastically.

*Oh. My. God.* I thought. How could I have been so stupid as to believe the client had thousands of headphones for the audience? Of course, the translation would not be simultaneous. I would say a sentence or two onstage and then wait for Dmitry to translate it.

Imagine if Robbie Williams was asked just before he went onstage to let every other song be sung by a Take That member (and one of the lesser-known ones at that).

I would have to Plan C this thing.

The audience started to make their way back into the arena. Hundreds of seats were filling up quickly.

But the presentation had finally landed on the computer behind the mixing desk. The Wi-Fi must have found a digital shortcut.

And then the laptop just died. The screen went blank.

"What the ... ?" I couldn't help cursing.

The technician looked over and sighed, "Battery dead ... sorry."

"Well, is there a cable to plug the laptop into a socket?"

"Left at office ... sorry," the technician replied.

This was bad.

In my talks, I have always concealed my lack of actual knowledge with really cool, funny and multimedia images.

Some speakers can deliver magic with nothing more than their voice and words.

I was not one of those speakers. I needed visuals, sounds and effects to dazzle the audience. Without them, I felt ... naked.

This was turning into that kind of nightmare. You are naked on a stage with nothing to say. And with Dmitry standing next to you, waiting to translate your nothingness to an audience of thousands of sales reps in an ice hockey arena.

The lights went down.

Music was playing.

The moderator onstage was babbling in a foreign language, but I managed to hear my name and the word meaning 'future.'

It was showtime.

Wearily, I made my way up the stairs with Dmitry in tow.

I had never been so frightened before a talk in my life.

I was going to crash and burn harder than I'd ever done before.

Only I didn't.

Through luck or willpower or karma, which I don't believe in, I delivered a masterpiece.

It wasn't really about anything. I opened the talk by proclaiming that I would give the audience five important ideas for the future.

As Dmitry was translating, I came up with the idea of dancing around him, making him part of the show.

I can't dance even if my life depends on it, but the goofy dad dance somehow connected with the crowd.

I made up the five important ideas as I went along. I delivered them slowly and with authority as if they had gravitas. In reality, the slow pace enabled me to think ahead about what could possibly come next.

It worked.

As we approached the end, I thought about how best to end the speech.

*Robbie Williams*, I thought to myself.

I'll do a sing-along of *Angels*.

*And when I sing about loving angels instead, I'll kiss the hand of the oldest woman I can spot in the audience*, I thought, pushing myself farther out on the ledge that this talk had become.

It worked.

Thousands of people were on their feet.

Dmitry and I embraced like we had been a dynamic duo for years.

People stopped me on the way from the stage to take selfies or ask for autographs.

My long-lost dreams of rock stardom had come true.

This was the best speech I had ever delivered.

Unfortunately, I had done it in Kyiv, Ukraine.

Only a few years later, Russia invaded the country, and Kyiv became a city under siege. I often thought about what happened to the people I had spoken to on that fateful day of the sales conference. And how meaning-less it seemed in the face of this new horror unfolding in Ukraine.

I delivered a really good speech.

In the worst possible location.

From a business perspective.

While entertaining Ukrainian sales reps might have a priceless spiritual value, it is not something you can eat or pay your bills with.

This book is not about giving good talks; it's about making money by giving talks – even mediocre ones.

# INTRODUCTION

# WHAT IS THE BUSINESS?

The evening was getting late, and my mouth had the sour aftertaste of red wine. I had been giving a dinner speech at an IT conference gala dinner. We were in a luxury hotel in London, and the dinner guests could be divided into two halves: those who had already left, deeming the hour late, and the next morning's appointments calling for an earlyish night; and those who stayed behind drinking whatever was left in wine glasses or calling for harder stuff at the bar.

I was somewhere in the middle, pondering my options, The Clash-style, of whether to stay or go.

That's when Dale leaned over. More California hippie than IT professional, Dale had founded a massively successful company and sold it for a lot of money a few years back. Now, he mainly drifted around the IT world, giving the odd talk and sharing his wisdom with whoever would listen.

"Hey, Magnus," he said in a raspy voice, betraying his appreciation of all things smokeable. "You don't make koi pond money, do ya?"

I must have looked thoroughly puzzled, which I was, but he did not wait for a response.

"You make a comfortable middle-class living doing what you do, right? But you don't make koi pond money."

"What exactly is koi pond money?" I asked, bewildered.

"It's my hobby," said Dale. "I breed koi fish and design ponds for them to swim around my gardens." Gardens. Plural.

I had once owned a fishbowl, but I was pretty sure that didn't count.

Dale was right. As a speaker, I make a comfortable middle-class living. But I didn't make koi pond money.[1]

Allow me to introduce myself. For over two decades, I have been travelling worldwide, giving talks about trendspotting and future thinking. I have written several books and hail from the near-Arctic kingdom of Sweden. I have been called its greatest export, next to ABBA and meatballs, by someone who once attended a seminar I spoke at in Manchester. This book has been written to help you – and myself – understand exactly why I've been paid exorbitant fees to give talks.

Why am I getting paid for speaking? And why has public speaking become a way to make a living, not just a pension boost for famous people and retired politicians? What, exactly, is the *business* of speaking?

---

1   For the record, koi fish can cost hundreds or thousands of dollars. Digging the pond and installing filtration systems will add another, say, 20 or 30 thousand. It's good if you have a sizeable garden for this and neighbours living far away as to not complain. Maintaining the pond and feeding the fish costs hundreds of dollars per month. It all adds up. If you don't have a couple hundred thousand dollars lying around and a garden measured in acres, koi pond design and koi breeding are not for you.

# MAKING MONEY
# – THE BASICS

Contrary to what it may sound and sometimes look like, business is not merely about keeping busy. It is the fine art and questionable science of making money by doing things for others. It can be done on a small or enormous scale, but at its heart, money changes hands because something has been done, made or created. No money, no business. If you want to make money doing something, it is a good idea to be aware of some basic tenets of business.

- Number One: Being good at something difficult is the best place to start if you want to make money. This is why good chefs and Adele can command high fees, but boiling an egg or singing karaoke will be done for free.

- Number Two: A professional – i.e., somebody who can make money from what they do – is good at doing the same thing for many different people. An amateur – the egg boiler or karaoke star – does different things for the same group of people.

- Number Three: Doing business is about understanding that everyone wants something ... to happen, to get somewhere, to come true and so on. Nobody is sitting around waiting to give you money, but everyone has a project they are working on, a problem – or many – they want to be solved or someplace – real or imagined – they want to get to. Understanding this need is key to having them part with their hard-earned cash. The late business professor Clayton Christensen put it as follows: "What job are you hiring a product or service to do for you?"

- Number Four: It is useless to be good at something if you cannot sell it.

- Number Five: If you cannot sell it, find somebody who can. I once interviewed the founder of fashion retailer H&M, who said the best advice for budding entrepreneurs is to hire your opposite. A brake pedal if you're constantly on the gas, a details-obsessed individual if you're a big-picture person, or somebody who can sell what you cannot.

- Number Six: It's not about you ... or what you feel. Passion is an asset in art or religion. Nobody cares if a plumber or flight controller is passionate ...

- Number Seven: ... but it's better to be charming than not. People prefer doing business with pleasant people rather than assholes.

- Number Eight: Just like the idea of eight tenets is arbitrary, doing business is not a precise science but a mix of the rational and irrational. Solving a rare disease is noble and profitable. Tying a bungee cord around someone's foot so they can jump off a cliff is less noble but still profitable. The point here is that business rules will always be somewhat fuzzy. It's open to grand endeavours and noble achievements but also to grifters, frauds and generally silly ideas.

Applying these principles to the business of speaking, we can establish the following:

- Number One: Standing on a stage in front of people is scary to some people, but it's not difficult. Standing on a stage and delivering a speech that will make people react – intellectually and/or emotionally – is difficult. Feeling sorry for the speaker does not count.

- Number Two: Politicians and CEOs tend to be good at speaking onstage. But they will always talk about new and different things. A professional speaker delivers the same talk – more or less – over and over again, all over the world.

- Number Three: It may look like the audience is there for the magnificent You (capital Y). They are not. In professional speaking, they have likely not paid out of their own pocket to see you. An events manager or CEO thought putting a speaker on the agenda would be a good idea. Prove them right.

- Number Four: Giving a good speech is selling a good speech.

- Number Five: Speaking is a solitary profession; you will need people on your side, not least for bookkeeping and paying taxes on time.

- Number Six: Social media feeds are full of trite superlatives from speakers who are 'excited,' 'super-proud' and 'passionate.' If you can't do a good job, nobody cares. If you do a good job, it doesn't matter if you are having fun doing it or going through horrible things in your private life.

- Number Seven: Being a speaker who makes money is not about being yourself. It is about crafting a sellable product.

- Number Eight: A book about the business side of speaking can never be more – or less – than the experience of somebody who has built a business out of public speaking. It's a fine art but questionable science.

On that note, let's examine what this book sets out to accomplish and avoid.

# THE S-WORD

'Success' often evokes a paradoxical blend of disdain and embarrassment. It's frequently spoken with a hint of irony, as if it's a shallow or gauche pursuit. Many hesitate to openly claim it, fearing it sounds arrogant or simplistic, while others view it with suspicion, equating it to materialism or superficial achievement. This ambivalence reflects our complex relationship with the concept – admiring its allure yet wary of its implications. To cut to the chase, a succinct definition of success is achieving one's goals, no matter how lofty or grounded they may be. In the business world, these goals are bound to – and should be – connected to money. No, money is not everything, but it is a sign that you are providing something people are willing to pay for. While life is certainly greater than business and cannot be reduced to a binary success/failure scale, business is an ongoing pursuit of goals, and money is the currency informing you whether these goals have been achieved.

# WHAT THIS BOOK
# IS AND IS NOT

*The Business of Speaking* is a book about how to make a decent – good – income from public speaking. It is not a book if you want to become a star. If you want to become a star, remember that fame is just a set of misunderstandings around a new name and thereby fleeting by nature.

Neither is it a book about building a company. Some speakers – we are looking at you, Tony Robbins – build an enterprise selling books, self-help courses and arcane rituals. This is not a book about getting rich. You won't earn koi pond money.

Most books about speaking are about how to craft a good speech and how to be a good speaker. That is a necessary but not sufficient means of building a business. And 'good' can mean many different things. *Macarena* and Taylor Swift topped the charts but have very different perceptions of quality. To say nothing about painters that died in poverty and were discovered decades later or music groups that have high cred but small audiences. The world is full of good things, whereas good business is rare.

This is a book for those who have had people tell them, "You're a good speaker," but have never been able to make money from it.

It's also a book for fellow speakers who want to feel they are not alone in the craziness of the profession. Or are looking to take it to the next level in terms of income.

Finally, it's an insight into one of the weirdest yet legal industries out there, so you may want to come along for the amusement.

# THE STRUCTURE OF THIS BOOK AND DISCLAIMERS

In the spirit of zany business logic, this book is structured like Biblical commandments ... because why not?

1. Thou shalt wander the earth and do a hundred bad speeches.

2. Thou shalt prioritize exposure over fees.

3. Thou shalt build a product, not a persona.

4. Thou shalt worship no other gods than nutritious turds.

5. Thou shalt practise the fine art of R&D.

6. Thou shalt treat other speakers with grace and generosity.

7. Thou shalt treat middlemen like insects.

8. Thou shalt only value the almighty dollar or euro or British pound.

9. Thou shalt understand that not all speaking engagements are created equal.

10. Thou shalt SHOW UP.

The Lord said to Moses, "Come up to me on the mountain and stay here, and I will give you the tablets of stone with the law and commandments I have written for their instruction," but the Bible does not specify how these divine principles were discovered. The commandments – not wanting to be sacrilegious, I have settled for nine – presented in this book were acquired through 20 years of travelling the world and giving talks. Sometimes making money. Sometimes having clients tell me to go to hell. This book is the scar tissue of these decades. And talking about scar tissue, I have a disclaimer before we begin: Don't become a speaker for a living!

It will screw up your relationships, your marriage and your self-image. It will make you neurotic, mildly narcissistic (unless you already suffer from severe narcissism, in which case it will be aggravated), and stuck on trains, planes, in taxis and in airports. "Do what you love, and you'll never work a day in your life" should read, "Do what you love, and you'll work super hard all the time without any boundaries and take everything too personally."

You have been warned.

Still here?

OK, let's learn how to make money as a speaker.

# THE FIRST
# COMMANDMENT

# THOU SHALT WANDER THE EARTH AND DO A HUNDRED BAD SPEECHES

*And they shall be the worst kind of bad because you felt they were pretty good. A couple of people even chuckled at your jokes and said hi afterwards. Trust me, the speech was bad. It was short on content, low on style, lacked finesse and offered little in either enlightenment or entertainment. Like believing you can write after cracking out a good blog post or two is self-delusion on a deep scale, believing you can offer anything good as a speaker before you've bombed a hundred times means you've been misinformed. The hundred bad speeches will be fun, though. A TedX middle of nowhere here, a boring bank conference there. You'll even get paid for some of these bad speeches. But they're bad, nevertheless.*

I could not believe how unreliably lucky I was. Blessed even. I was getting paid for my first speaking assignment ever. On my way, by train, to Karlstad, a university town in the midwest of Sweden, to speak at the opening of a museum exhibition. It was Tuesday. Spring was in the air. The train wheels hammered rhythmically against the rails, like an upbeat drum loop to my good spirits. I had not been the museum's first choice. But my journalist friend, who had been asked by the museum curator to speak, had simply deferred and told me to go in his place. *Man, was he missing out*, I thought to myself as the landscape sped by outside the train window.

I was on my way, literally and figuratively.

When I arrived at the museum, it was deathly empty. But I was early, and the crowds would probably arrive soon. I said hello to the museum staff, set up my laptop, attached a lapel mic and did some jumping jacks to get warmed up. I felt like an athlete slash rock star. This presentation would take everybody by storm.

Some time went by, and ... where was everybody? The opening was due to begin in 15 minutes and, not counting the staff, I counted one sole visitor. And he was asking where the toilet was.

The curator shrugged apologetically and said that the museum had put up loads of posters at the university in the hope that some students would show up.

I wondered if there was any place on earth where students would prioritize going to a museum exhibition en masse on a Tuesday afternoon.

The emptiness of the empty museum was emphasized by the silence punctuated by the ticking of a large clock.

If a speech is given to nobody, is it even a speech?

Tick.

Tock.

Suddenly, the doors swung open.

Finally, a group of people showed up.

They were not necessarily the target audience of my presentation, but since the speech was due to start in only a few minutes, I urged them to take their seats.

The presentation could begin.

Over 20 individuals sat in front of me. All from the local primary school. Nobody above the age of nine. Apart from the teacher, who kept telling the children to be quiet.

She also forewarned me that they would have to leave to catch the bus back to school within a half hour, which would be about halfway through my speech.

I feverishly tried to catch the children's attention with my PowerPoint slides.

They were more interested in a squirrel running outside the window.

As promised, they all got up and left when I still had half my presentation left to give.

The room was again empty.

Bar for the toilet-seeking patron from before who had fallen asleep at the back of the room.

I slowly realized why the more experienced journalist friend had turned this opportunity down.

At least I got paid, one could argue.

But I didn't necessarily get paid in the monetary sense of the word.

I got a second-class return train ticket and a free museum entrance. I decided to stay optimistic and consider it a speaking fee.

The train back was cancelled, so I took a six-hour bus ride home instead.

The oft-repeated words of supermodels echoed in my head: "It's not as glamorous as you think."

I started speaking in the early 2000s, and for the first half-decade, I had dozens upon dozens of these kinds of endeavours.

There was the insurance company that wanted 25% of their fee back because I finished 15 minutes early in a one-hour speech (they had specifically asked for 45 minutes to leave time for Q&A).

There was the Danish company that refused to pay me because they felt I had insulted them (they were seven white men in a board meeting, and I had just told them to start thinking about diversity).

There was the Slovenian advertising festival, where I improvised a speech based on a conversation I'd had during lunch. Improvisation is good. But not for paid engagements. I also tried to cry on command when reciting a poem at said Slovenian festival. An ill-considered experiment. Poetry, in general, makes for sluggish keynote speeches. Especially when not delivered in the audience's native tongue.

A speech for SAAB Automobile's workers was booked well in advance. Although the company had gone bankrupt, the organizer thought it would be a good idea for me to come and speak anyway.

It was not a good idea.

And so on.

When the renowned actor Cillian Murphy was nominated and subsequently won an Oscar for the movie *Oppenheimer*, he quoted a film director who said, "It takes 30 years to make an actor."

Well, it takes at least a hundred bad speeches to make a speaker.

# STANDING ON
# THE SHOULDERS
# OF SCREW-UPS

Career evolution happens by elimination. We become what we don't fail at in life. I was a reluctant business school graduate who dreamed of making movies in Hollywood. So naturally, I wrote a novel that nobody wanted to publish and can best be described as 'interesting' (pronounced with a hint of distaste). I started a rock band that never got past the dreaded Bermuda Triangle in the audience (wherein the space in front of the stage is left empty throughout the show as most patrons hover closer to the bar area in the back – a sign as good as any that your band is not a draw). I enrolled in a film course and dropped out. I tried journalism and dropped out. In short, nothing was working. I threw stuff at a wall to see what would stick, and everything crashed to the floor with a thud. I discovered professional speaking in the shambles left on the floor. I pared some of my storytelling ambitions with wannabe rock stardom. I mixed in some basic business school lessons and blended in some journalistic perspectives. I initially called myself a futurist but was soon told that the futurists were Italian fascist poets in the 1920s.

Since I was neither Italian nor fascist nor dead, I proudly stole a title I came across at British Telecom: 'futurologist.' A cheap way of making what I did sound somewhat scientific (did I mention that I applied for a PhD at my alma mater? No? Well, they wouldn't take me on. Years later, I heard bestselling author Malcolm Gladwell explain why he never did a PhD: "Because academics are hedgehogs, and I'm a fox." I stole that excuse too). Anyway, nothing happened when I'd put all these things together – the title, the aspirations, the basic tenements – like dressing up a paper doll. I gave my first speech for free in the winter of 2003. I even paid money to do it. I rented a small studio space, bought beer and sandwiches, rented a projector to show slides and sent invitations by snail mail. A dozen people showed up, possibly because they were friends with nothing better to do on a Monday evening and saw a chance for a free meal. I got zero referrals and paid speaking engagements, but I got a few pats on the back and thank-you notes.

I did the same thing a year later. Just over a dozen people showed up. Same end result.

Throughout these years, I held day jobs to pay bills. Cat litter salesperson, lottery ticket distributor, PowerPoint secretary and media researcher. Nothing fancy. Little fun. But jobs to sustain my dream of making it as a speaker.

And I had absolutely zero doubt … that I would fail at this too.

No confidence whatsoever.

Then, in my third year of hosting my now-annual evening of free sandwiches and random musings about ideas, trends and the future, something happened: more people showed up.

And then, a year later, I had to change to a larger venue.

It cost a fortune, but for the first time, I received some kind of acknowledgment that something I did was working. It was a blip on the radar screen. Out of a series of failures, something promising had been born.

I had become a blip.

# LONG AND HARD
# IS THE ROAD

You cannot live off being a blip. Blipping does not put food on the table or pay off a mortgage. But it is a clue that the path you are on is, at least, the right one. Then comes a slow, hard realization. Learning is linear. Behind those three academic-sounding words lies an uncomfortable truth: it will take a lot of time to go from being a blip to making a living from speaking. It will take time, and you will fail.

And they will often be the worst kind of failures, in that you thought things were going quite well until you learned otherwise, like falling can feel like flying.

What you are passing through are the four stages of competence. Imagine for a moment that your speaking career is a computer game in which you must master each level to advance to the next.

# LEVEL ONE:
# UNCONSCIOUS INCOMPETENCE

When you start speaking, you don't know how bad you are. Let's return to the insurance company that wanted 25% of their fee back because I finished 15 minutes early in a one-hour speech. Here's what happened. I had put on my coolest outfit – ahem, a red shirt with a black tie, making me look like a kind of matador. I had crammed my coolest, funniest slides into a speech, ready to rock and roll.

I was about to speak in front of 100 female secretaries at an insurance company.

Being unconsciously incompetent at the time, here's what I was not aware of.

Don't be weird if you're a man speaking in front of women. Be sexy. Be George Clooney. Be a Hollywood leading man. Be self-deprecating. Be slow and gentle. Dressing as a matador is ill-advised.

If you're a business school graduate about to speak in front of secretaries, make <u>them</u> feel smart. Don't just mindlessly hammer away at PowerPoint slides. Invite them into a conversation.

Finally, don't do things at warp speed to cover up whatever shortcomings your red shirt and funky slides try to cover up. Slow it down; make it simple. Breathe.

I knew none of this at the time. When the client wanted their money back, it was not because of time; it was because my talk sucked. And I did not know.

If you cannot fathom having people judge what you do harshly and honestly, public speaking simply is not for you. You don't have to like it, but you have to accept it.

## LEVEL TWO: CONSCIOUS INCOMPETENCE

When I entered a room full of recently laid-off workers at SAAB Automobile, I realized immediately that this would not go well. I was presented as a very successful speaker who had flown into this small town in Sweden the same morning from my home in Stockholm, the capital. Most countries have a lot of skepticism toward the (real and perceived) arrogance of the people from their capital city. In other words, I began way below zero. And I had no tools at my disposal to climb up from there. If you're the essence of a white-collar worker – with a posh, plummy accent from the nation's capital – you cannot win over a room full of blue-collar workers recently laid off. It had been a mistake to agree to this event, but I had made my bed and would lie in it. I was counting down each minute of my talk. The audience and I could not wait for me to get off the stage and fly back to wherever I came from.

I knew I sucked. A step up from the false beliefs I held at the gathering of insurance secretaries.

# LEVEL THREE:
# CONSCIOUS COMPETENCE

The first two levels constitute at least a hundred talks. You read that right; you will give a hundred bad talks during your linear learning journey. Then one day, you will stand on a stage, feel the wind in your hair and a little voice echoing in your head: "I do not suck anymore."

For me, it happened at a pharmaceutical summit. I was so used to the audience's disharmony that I did not stop to check on them. I went through the motions, delivered my lines and showed off my slides. Everyone rose in a standing ovation when the talk ended – my first ever.

I was dumbfounded. Where did this come from? Why had they been so kind? Had everything else on the agenda been so bad that they celebrated mere mediocrity? Things that had been working against me for so long suddenly worked for me.

Like the proverbial ugly duckling, I was not used to being a swan. I felt no pride or accomplishment – just a sense of wonder. Reaching your moment of conscious competence is a miracle to behold. Alas, it does not last, so savour it while you can.

# LEVEL FOUR:
## UNCONSCIOUS COMPETENCE

The visionary communications theorist Marshall McLuhan once said, "The 'expert' is the man who stays put." Disregarding the gendered language for a moment, he has a point. Once you reach the third stage – being aware that you are a good speaker – it's tempting to move further, develop new angles, or leave the business altogether in the name of "been there, done that."

Yet, true mastery takes time. And the goalposts keep moving.

When I had been speaking professionally for more than a decade, a global pandemic made events freeze up, and speeches were expected to be delivered virtually on Zoom, Teams or Webex. It was Day One all over again. From having mastered the ability to deliver speeches in vast auditoriums, everything had to be relearned. Merely adjusting the physical speeches to a tiny screen did not work. You had to redesign everything: the delivery, the message and the method.

Unconscious competence is the ability to readjust and adapt to new circumstances. You will be unaware of it before you face it. In a long career – in the pursuit of mastery – it is bound to happen repeatedly.

# FIND YOUR *IKIGAI*

Anyone can make a living as a speaker.

Yet almost no one does.

Read that statement again. Anyone. Almost no one.

The speaker profession has room for anyone or anything. Diversity is an issue in other industries, but it is the very reason for being in the speaking world. A transgender Native American mixing anthropological research with punk rock music might have a hard time getting a job in a bank but would easily give talks for a high fee in no time.

Anyone can make a living as a speaker.

But actually doing it is rare, and the reason is *ikigai*, an ancient Japanese concept popularized by Mieko Kamiya in her 1966 book, *On the Meaning of Life*. Take a moment to study the chart below to understand the four components of finding your *ikigai*.

Glossophobia – the intense fear of public speaking –
means that not everyone will be thrilled by the idea of
delivering a talk in front of others. But many people
do. They take every chance at dinner parties, birth-
days and weddings to raise their voice, raise a toast or
raise an issue. Some even love it. That doesn't mean
they have a chance of getting paid for it. And if we're
talking about in-laws, aunts and uncles, just because
they like rambling at the family get-together doesn't
mean they are good at it. This is why 'stuff you like
doing' is the weakest link in finding your *ikigai*. Look

for something other people think you are good at. As I described earlier, my novel writing and rock music compositions had limited appeal. They had no appeal whatsoever.

Yet even if people like what you do, its commercial potential may be severely limited. We have all come across fantastically talented street musicians or bar singers. Few of them were able to go from busking to selling out stadiums. Ed Sheeran is the only one that comes to mind. And even if people might be open to paying you, few will from the very start. Going from being good at something to earning a living from it takes time, and later chapters will explore exactly what this route entails. Yet, organizing your future career according to the four fields of *ikigai* will enable you to ask the right questions. Can I make a living from this? Is my heart – and head – in it? What are others telling me to do with my life? And so forth.

Find one job that fits well enough into most of the areas.

Focus on that one job.

Find something you can do for a long time.

The expert is the one who stays put.

# CONCLUSION: FIRST ATTEMPT IN LEARNING

It is often said that we live in exponential times. Computer power, stock market movements and fashion trends all move at great speed.

Nevertheless, human learning is still linear. It takes place one small step after another. You will stumble many times before you can stand upright.

Learning is lonely. You have to go through the stages of incompetence and explore the paths to *ikigai* on your own.

Most importantly, learning is painful. Or, to rephrase, pain is the greatest teacher. It is when you fail, feel ashamed or misunderstood that real learning takes place. How on earth could my result fall so far away from my goal? Why are others succeeding at this when I don't? Am I cursed or merely unlucky? Even if you keep climbing the four stages of incompetence, some of these questions still linger. That is the real lesson. Just like building muscle requires lifting heavier weights continuously, a slight sense of insufficiency is bound to haunt you. Am I good enough? Can I somehow change my talk or speaking style to do it differently, maybe even better? And so on.

The next chapter is about balancing exposure – to get through your hundred bad talks – with money. It is not just about finding your fit and getting good at speaking. It is about getting paid.

**DO!**     Embrace the Failure:
Dive headfirst into every
opportunity to speak, regardless
of how small or seemingly
insignificant. Each failure is a
stepping stone toward mastery.
The path to becoming a
compelling speaker is paved
with a hundred bad speeches.

 **DON'T!**  Avoid the Spotlight:
Don't shy away from speaking
engagements because of fear
of failure or embarrassment. If
you're not willing to risk bombing,
you'll never reach the heights of
speaking success. Avoidance is
the enemy of growth.

 **DO!**     Learn and Adapt:
Continuously refine your
craft based on the feedback
and experiences from your
speeches. Treat every audience
reaction as valuable data for
improvement. Use every bad
speech as a lesson.

**DON'T!** Stay in Your Comfort Zone:
Don't stick to what feels
safe or familiar. Challenging
yourself with diverse audiences
and topics is crucial. Staying
comfortable means staying
mediocre.

 **DO!** Find Your *Ikigai*:
Align your speaking topics with
what you love, what you're good
at, what the world needs, and
what you can be paid for. Strive
to find that sweet spot where
passion meets profession.

 **DON'T!** Ignore Feedback:
Don't dismiss criticism or feedback
from your audience. Ignoring these
insights will stall your progress and
prevent you from becoming the
speaker you're meant to be.

**DO!**   Stay Persistent:
Keep pushing forward despite
setbacks. Building a speaking
career is a marathon, not a
sprint. Persistence is key to
transitioning from a blip on the
radar to a full-fledged expert.

   Rush the Process:
Don't expect overnight success.
The journey to becoming a
great speaker is long and
often gruelling. Patience and
perseverance are essential.

# THE SECOND
# COMMANDMENT

# THOU SHALT PRIORITIZE EXPOSURE OVER FEES

*Fees boost your ego and bank account. Exposure increases your speaking ability and brand recognition. Too high a fee will mean very little exposure, to the detriment of your ability and wallet. Ensure you do between 30 and 100 (yes, you read that right) talks annually and see fees as a welcome bonus. You can even speak for free if the setting is right.*

Richard Branson is genuinely nice in real life, a trait not all celebrities share. Backstage at a central London conference venue, I found him to be open, warm and friendly. He readily posed for photographs and cracked jokes with the staff.

For me, the nervousness was palpable. After all, I was about to open for him with a 5-minute monologue, a prestigious yet daunting task. Sir Richard's jokes only mildly eased my tension.

Then, a knock on the door signalled it was showtime. And that's when it hit me: I was utterly unprepared. This realization brought to mind U2's Joshua Tree tour in the late 1980s. Their album was selling so well that their management booked 50,000-seat stadiums, not 10,000-seat areas. But they did not have enough hit songs to entertain a stadium for two hours, so Bono Vox, their lead singer, would have to sell every song by doing physical stunts like running around inside the stadium or climbing lighting rigs. I was about to face a vast audience with scant recognizable material, and I knew I had to make each moment count, possibly with my own version of 'acrobatics.'

I grabbed a half-empty (or was it half-full?) bottle of Diet Coke on my way to the stage, thinking it could serve as some kind of prop.

I untucked my (stylistically ill-advised) Matador-style red shirt, loosened my tie and opened the collar.

I sought some punk-business hybrid look.

I had to do something to stand out and make a dent. The audience expected one of the world's greatest entrepreneurs, not a random Swedish futurologist.

The stage manager lightly tapped me on the shoulder.

It was time.

The speech was a blur.

Thousands of people were waiting for Branson.

They looked at me with quiet reserve or outright boredom but, in some rare instances, a slight look of amusement.

Something I did registered with them.

All I remember is that I gave the half-empty Coke bottle to a gentleman in the front row as a giveaway. "Skål! (Cheers)," he replied as if raising a toast.

My five minutes were up.

Exiting the stage, I considered it another addition to my list of unsuccessful talks – or so I thought.

# ESCAPE VELOCITY

In physics, escape velocity is the speed something needs to reach to break free from a planet's or moon's gravity and not fall back. In the speaker business, it is the momentum needed to break away from the pack of anonymity and establish yourself as a trusted supplier of keynote talks. The fuel needed for escape velocity is gained by saying yes – to everything. Just get out there. Learn before you earn. Don't second-guess, plan or strategize. Nobody will pay you much before they know you're a safe bet. And you will not be a safe bet before you have been baptized by a hundred bad talks. I gave free talks to schools, universities, advertising agencies, theatre groups, museums and other monetary-challenged institutions. It was a good deal for both. I got to practise. They got free, mediocre infotainment.

Besides learning, all these yeses aim to expose yourself to the enigmatic powers of serendipity. After a few years, I got a last-minute inquiry from a temp agency to come and speak at their leadership meeting.

They had planned for one of Sweden's most sought-after speakers on the topics of trends, future thinking and leadership, but he had been caught with his pants down – literally – procuring sexual services, which is illegal in Sweden. Somebody among the temp agency's managers had seen me speak at a museum and liked what she heard. One thing led to another, and the meeting went so well that the company decided to host a Nordic roadshow on "Jobs of the Future," with me as the star billing. A free talk given in a museum, combined with the poor judgment of the intended speaker, led to a 30-date paid tour in Sweden, Finland, Denmark and Norway. Whenever you read about how entrepreneurs and inventors of pop stars succeeded, it always comes down to the power of serendipity – random events positively conspiring for you.

# THE SIRENS IN THE SPOTLIGHT

The spotlight in show business – and yes, public speaking is showbusiness – is deceptive. You can easily get blinded by it and believe it is all about you and what a superstar you are. To steer clear of that delusion, let's reexamine the journey taken above and analyse it using two of the basic tenets of business outlined in the Introduction:

- Being good at something difficult is the best place to start if you want to make money.

  › It's easy to believe that giving a talk is the hard part. It's not. The hardest part is giving a talk when you don't feel like it, like when you face a room of thousands eager to hear Sir Richard Branson, and your only job is interrupting the proceedings. The same goes for writers, chefs and professional athletes, to name a few. It is not doing the job in and of itself that will enable you to make a living – it is your ability to do it when all other conditions are dire. This book is about the business – not the joy – of speaking.

- Doing business is about understanding that everyone wants something ... to happen, get somewhere, come true and so on.

  › The manager at the temp agency wanted to solve a problem: who could quickly replace the booked speaker so that nobody would complain? In this case, it is not about being a particularly good speaker – you only have to be good enough – but about being someone who can say yes quickly and help them solve the problem. Compare it to your toilet leaking on a Friday night. You don't care if the plumber who can help you is nice or passionate. You don't care if they are particularly good at plumbing as long as they solve the problem and prevent the toilet from leaking. Understanding what the other wants to happen is key to doing business.

Your hundred yeses build awareness of you as a speaker and help you understand how and where your services fit in. You start with a distorted sense of omnipotence – which is why you will fail so often – but slowly learn what niche best suits your abilities.

# CONCLUSION: CREAM SWIMMING

Wonky marketeers call it URL, an acronym for Ubiquity First, Revenues Later. They mean you must build broad awareness and market penetration before the money starts flowing in. My late grandfather, not a marketeer, called it Cream Swimming. He explained that swimming long enough in cream makes it solid enough to climb out of the bowl. The yes-years are Cream Swimming. You do many engagements to raise visibility and build your brand. You also extend your brand's reach, not just more of the same kind of conferences. Above all, they expose you to serendipity. I got to open for Richard Branson because I had taught a course in trendspotting for journalists in Stockholm, one of which was from Lithuania, so they invited me to speak at a conference in Vilnius, where I shared the stage with a marketing guru from London who introduced me to his speaking agent in London who wanted to test what I could do so he put me onstage in front of Branson. Phew. All careers, no matter what profession, look like this. One thing leads to the next. In Hollywood, they say that you need two things to succeed:

information and relationships. If you have one, you will get the other.

Somebody filmed part of the talk I held before Branson –'talk' is a generous word; the French have a better word, *intervention* – and put it on a new website called YouTube. It was merely two minutes of grainy footage, but it featured my name, with the title 'Futurologist,' and Richard Branson.

After a few months, a Belgian bank reached out. They were about to merge with their Dutch counterpart and needed somebody to come and talk about the future of banking and finance. Would I be interested? And by the way, they needed somebody to come and join them at over 20 sessions to enable all managers and leaders of the future entity to listen.

What I thought was another addition to my list of unsuccessful talks had landed me at the next level in speaking.

I now faced a daunting task. How would I find an interesting enough talk to engage senior finance leaders in over 20 sessions? The next chapter is about finding consistency as a speaker, the basis of doing business.

**DO!**      Prioritize Exposure:
Say yes to every speaking
opportunity, regardless of the
fee. Exposure will enhance your
speaking skills and increase your
brand recognition. Aim for 30 to
100 talks annually, even if many
are unpaid.

 **DON'T!**    Chase High Fees:
Don't prioritize high fees at the
expense of exposure. High fees
with limited gigs will stunt your
growth as a speaker. Focus on
getting out there and honing
your craft.

 **DO!**      Seize Serendipity:
Embrace unexpected
opportunities and random
events that come your way.
These can often lead to
significant breakthroughs and
new connections. Be open to
the power of serendipity.

**DON'T!** Get Blinded by the Spotlight:
Don't let the allure of high-profile events inflate your ego.
Remember, it's about building consistent, reliable performance,
not basking in the glory of one-off successes.

 **DO!** Solve Problems:
Understand that your role is to solve the audience's or event organizer's problems, whether it's filling a slot last-minute or engaging a difficult crowd. Be the reliable solution they need.

 **DON'T!** Ignore the Hard Parts:
Don't underestimate the difficulty of performing when conditions aren't ideal. The true test of a speaker is delivering a great talk even when the circumstances are tough.

**DO!**   Build Relationships: Cultivate connections with everyone you meet at your talks. Information and relationships are crucial to success. Networking can open doors to future opportunities.

 **DON'T!**   Wait for Perfect Conditions: Don't hold back until everything is just right. Dive in and adapt as you go. Perfect conditions rarely exist, and waiting for them will only delay your progress.

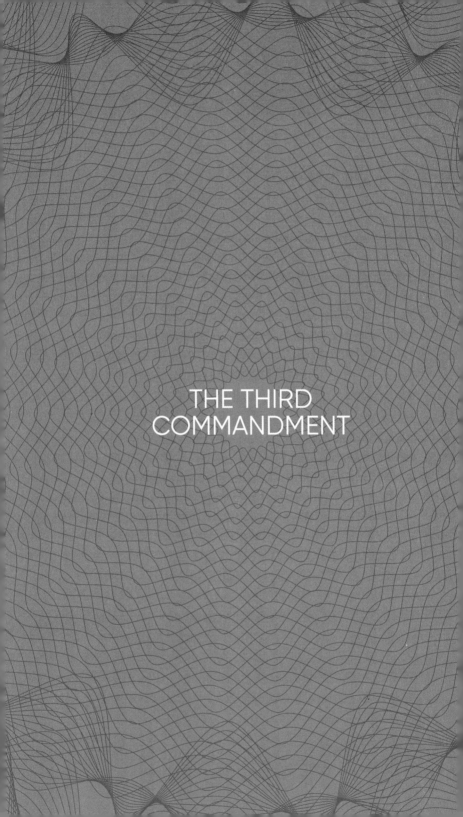

THE THIRD
COMMANDMENT

# THOU SHALT BUILD A PRODUCT, NOT A PERSONA

*Your speech is a 43- to 72-minute lump of coal that you should polish into a diamond over many years. It shall be witty, interesting, motivational, inspirational and multimedial. And there shall only be one. Not three different talks. No workshops. No moderator gigs. Nothing but the monolith talk that is as versatile as a McDonald's burger. Because your talk is so brilliantly perfect, people will assume you're equally perfect and brilliant. They will invite you to parties, follow you on Instagram, give you awards, ask you to sit on award juries, ask you to endorse stuff and so on. You should decline every one of these invitations since you're neither perfect nor brilliant. You're just a flawed, jaded, cynical bastard ... a human being, in other words. Let the product – the speech – speak for itself (!) so you can keep being an average Joe or Joanne.*

Something is to be said for playing Blitzkrieg Bop on a ukulele in front of a hundred drunk Samsung salespeople. It is one of those things that could either go splendidly or crash and burn completely. This was firmly in the latter camp. But it was more of a thud than a crash. Awkward could best describe the atmosphere. How did I get there?

As my speaking career had gone from a hundred bad freebie talks to getting some commercial traction, I had been asked to do a Scandinavian roadshow to help launch a new Samsung smartphone. "We would also like to give your book to all participants," said the eager project manager, which greatly flattered me. The only problem was that I had not yet written a book. It existed only as a sketch. In my head. To compensate, I suggested we give out ukuleles instead with the hazy logic that it symbolized the creative potential unlocked on a mass scale by the new phone. To my astonishment, the project manager agreed, and hundreds of ukuleles were shipped to Oslo, Stockholm and Copenhagen. My idea was that the end of my talk could be a collective singalong to a punk rock anthem and that I could smash my ukulele onstage. What could possibly go wrong? I would have venues across Scandinavia full of enthusiastic salespeople ready to pogo along. Fast forward to Oslo a few weeks later, on a drizzly Tuesday evening in October. Just under a hundred salespeople, all below the age of 25, were gathered and drank copious amounts of alcohol to offset the dreary weather outside. The country manager walked up onstage and gave a lacklustre presentation about sales stats and market support. This was followed by one of those bland, globally produced commercials about the new phone, and then it was time for yours truly to shine. The ukulele moment was to be the denouement to the climax of the evening. The cherry on the icing on the cake, so to speak. This was my time! I alone would help Samsung sales staff reach stratospheric highs in their potential, and tonight, Oslo would become a global showcase for Korean multinationals for how to do proper product launches.

The response was lukewarm at best. They looked at me with the facial expression you have when studying exotic animals at a zoo and trying to figure out what they are and what they are doing.

Had I stopped before the impromptu ukulele singalong, I think the common verdict would have been "Meh."

But I bravely soldiered on and put on my best ukulele rock-show performance. Hey ho, let's go!

The look went from watching an exotic animal to passing a smouldering car wreck on the motorway.

The atmosphere was one of "WTF?!"

As the song ended, I smashed the mini-guitar against the stage floor and held it aloof.

There was some scattered applause in the piercing silence.

I walked off the stage and tried to high-five the country manager. She left me hanging.

The next day's email put it succinctly: "Not good."

All speakers need a hit song. Something that gets people buzzing and talking long after you have left the stage. Something you can always fall back on, even as trends and conference themes shift. The search for a hit is equally long and arduous. You are bound to awkwardly smash up ukuleles at Norwegian sales meetings time and time again. Literally and figuratively.

# QUALITY
# IS BINARY

In the 1979 comedy *The Jerk*, Steve Martin plays a happy-go-lucky simpleton who moves to the big city to try his luck. Before he leaves the small family farm, his father shares some advice about success. He points to a pile of cow dung and says, "Shit!" Then to some shoe polishing cream and says, "'Shinola.'² If you can tell the difference, you'll find success." Martin carefully repeats the words 'shit' and 'Shinola' to great comedic effect. Hidden behind this joke is a deeper truth: people are binary regarding their view of quality. A movie is either good or bad. An advertisement either works or does not. A joke is funny or not. No amount of careful explanation will get the joke working if you do not laugh. In fact, having to explain a joke defeats its purpose. And yes, the speech at the Samsung sales conference was shit, not Shinola. So, how do you get from one to the other?

Engineers call it an MVP – a minimum viable product – and it describes something that is not perfect but good enough to get the job done. Your first mission as a speaker is to craft an MVP.

Your only guide on that journey is the audience and how it reacts. Cringeworthy ukulele shows, I learned, will be characterized as shit. Terms like 'weird,' 'complicated,' 'low energy' or the dreaded 'nice, I guess' are all synonyms with 'shit!' and when they appear on evaluations, it's a sign that you're still striving to find an MVP. Until expressions like 'really good,' 'amazing' or 'best I've ever heard' appear, you don't have a minimum viable product to make a living as a professional speaker. So, what does an MVP need to contain, and how do you get there?

---

2   A now-defunct brand of American shoe polishing cream

# THE KAIZEN
# OF SPEAKING

There is a common delusion among the self-employed, whether you are a freelance designer or public speaker: if you do good enough work, you will get good clients. In reality, the inverse is true: if you get good clients, you will get a chance to do good work. I could have delivered a speech worthy of the Louvre in the near-empty museum in Karlstad, and it would have gotten me nowhere. Now, I had 20 sessions booked with the leadership cadre at two banks in which to hone and practise my craft. After every session, I got written feedback explaining exactly how the content was received, what worked and what did not. It enabled me to continuously chisel away at the talk – deleting, honing and adjusting. Toyota coined this process *Kaizen*, which means continuous improvement. It is an evolutionary process wherein the redundant parts are removed, and working parts strengthened. As opposed to a scattershot approach where you randomly experiment or, as the American idiom goes, throw spaghetti at the wall to see if it sticks.

The audience and their reactions decide what works in a talk – not you. There may be things in there that you love and will want to keep, but if they don't go down well with the people listening, they have to go. The message would have been different if this book had been about rhetorical brilliance or political activism by giving speeches. In those instances, you are told to speak from the heart, emphasize certain messages and ensure everybody understands you. If, on the other hand, you want to make money by giving speeches, you have to take your ego out of the equation and build a product like Toyota made cars. Remember one of the tenets of business: it's not about you ... or what you feel.

Don't be yourself. You may be fun or boring, strange or normal (or what stand-up comedians call "an alien or a neighbour"), but when it comes to crafting a commercially viable talk, these things do not matter. What matters is the slightly duller concept of consistency.

# ABOVE ALL,
# BE CONSISTENT

When people brainstorm about organizing events, they tend to gravitate toward the spectacular: "Let's have a Moulin Rouge-themed ballroom with a futuristic edge and invite Nobel prize winners and former presidents to speak." Fame, in the spectacular sense, is often gained from notoriety. The semi-alcoholic French sex-obsessed novelist is more famous than his quiet, diligent counterpart, who churns out mystery novels every other year according to a preset formula. If you want fame, emulate the Frenchman. If you want to build a steady business, be reliable.

Consider cars as a parallel. You don't send an Italian sports car to pick VIPs up from the airport. Ferraris and Lamborghinis are sexy, but they swerve off the road if you press the gas pedal too hard. And the engine might not even start if the temperature is too low. And the noise of their running engines is unbearable to some. Italian sports cars are objects of affection and collectors' items, but in the business of VIP airport transfers, you will always use a boring but reliable Mercedes or BMW.

It is tempting to believe that, as a speaker, you are fundamentally different from a limousine driver. Wrong. You are both in the service industry and paid to perform a specific task. A limousine company would never send an Italian sports car.

To do good business as a speaker, build a reliable speech, not a persona. I've seen rock stars and Nobel prize winners fail spectacularly when they gave a speech but heard absolute gold from people who could best be described as slightly geeky.

Be selfless. Focus on crafting the speech.

Should you write a book? Should you have a TikTok channel or LinkedIn blog with a million followers? Should you be doing TV, etc.? The blunt answer is no, unless you think it's a lot of fun. The only thing that continuously sells a good speech is continuously delivering a good speech.

Anything can be sold once. Selling something over and over again is the real challenge.

# THE SELF-HARM OF GOOD INTENTIONS

"Be consistent" is deceptively simple advice. You will be bored in no time, and that's when the trouble starts. Idle hands are the devil's workshop, as the religiously devout are prone to repeat. Research by the Fraunhofer Institute in Germany showed that many innovations occurred when people were on training courses – but really bad training courses. They were away from the normal work environment, and the course was bad, so their minds wandered, and their creativity became supercharged. Similarly, as you travel around and give the same talk time after time, you slowly become bored and start trying new things. After all, you, too, want to be creative and innovative and not risk falling into the "same old, same old" mould. Or you may want to be important – a speaker somebody takes seriously, just like the activists and politicians whose rhetorical skills move mountains and earn them accolades and awards.

Remember that innovation is at the opposite end of quality assurance.

When you try new things, you have no idea how they will be received.

Your eagerness to invent or change your message becomes a kind of self-harm by good intentions. Instead of sticking with what works, you become unreliable – like the alcoholic French novelist or Italian sports car.

Instead of being selfless, you believe that your own mental stimulation is more important than what the audience is feeling and thinking.

Do not misunderstand – renewal is important in the long run, but just like research laboratories are hidden far away from consumer channels, trying out new material should happen far away from the paid speaking circuit. Get a few friends together in a room, get feedback, or do free conversational seminars with the expressed purpose that you are there to experiment.

When Canadian psychologist Jordan B. Peterson became a global superstar in the late 2010s, he booked a speaking tour with the goal that every evening would be different, depending on what he felt like talking about on that particular date.

In Stockholm, Sweden, I witnessed a sold-out arena with an audience ready to be dazzled and a rambling mess onstage.

# CREATE A MCTALK

McDonald's is underrated when it comes to innovation. They are often viewed with slight disdain for their junk food and used as a symbol for a kind of global sameness disease, sometimes called McDonaldization. Leaving any nutritional shortcomings aside, the critics fail to credit the company for its versatility. It has gone global by being able to cater to local tastebuds and culinary customs. In Norway, it serves McSalmon; in India, its burgers are vegetarian or chicken-based; in Japan, there is a Teriyaki burger. And so on. It can do this thanks to the service concept being modular. A burger is made from bread, sauce, protein and salad. The restaurant comprises several stations, from drinks and ice cream to burger making and fryers. In a modular concept, you can easily remove and replace some parts.

Your talk should be equally modular.

This is partly so that you can easily adjust it for time – sometimes you will be asked to speak for 20 minutes, at other times for nearly an hour – and partially so that you can adjust it for different themes, settings and audiences without compromising consistency.

When an HR audience asks you to speak, have a McHR-talk ready. Change the modules to tone things down in a more conservative setting, but let it rip when you present in Las Vegas.

McSales, McCFO, McGeneralInspiration, you get the point.

These should not be wholly different talks but variations around the same road-tested core. You spent those years doing bad talks and saying yes to everything to have a finely honed modular talk – a hit song – that does not rely solely on one joke, message or example.

# CONCLUSION: IT'S NOT ABOUT YOU

When you eventually start giving good talks, people will compliment you and assume you are as brilliant as the talk you just delivered. Since they haven't seen all the years you spent smashing up ukuleles in Oslo or feverishly tried to get near-empty museums fired up, they will assume you're naturally gifted. They will invite you to parties, ask you to sit on panels and interview you for magazines. Say yes if you have nothing better to do but be aware that none of these activities will propel your speaking career longevity. Only the quality of your talk – the actual product – will ensure that.

When companies organize conferences, the costs are gigantic. Venue, equipment, food and beverage, service staff – the numbers quickly reach stratospheric highs. If you add the indirect costs – people not being at their day job, travelling to and from the event, stuff people could have done with their time instead of being at the conference – even a small event costs large sums to arrange.

A speaker is merely another supplier to the event, like the lamps onstage, the coffee machine in the lobby or the name badge printer. You would not accept cold coffee, a dark stage, misprinted name badges or a sub-par keynote speech.

Be reliable, consistent, and ... Do. Not. Suck![3]

Or, to clarify, make a reliable, consistent and good talk so that you can continue living as a flawed human being like everyone else.

Thou shalt build a product, not a persona.

3   This particular piece of American advice was given to me before I
    gave a post-dinner speech to a group of CEOs. Alas, my talk ended up
    stinking to the high heavens. Nevertheless, the lesson was invaluable.
    Be good – preferably brilliant – instead of sucking!

**DO!** Build a Polished, Versatile Talk: Focus on creating a single, outstanding talk that you refine over time. Ensure it is witty, interesting, motivational, inspirational and multimedia-rich. This polished product will serve as your calling card and the cornerstone of your speaking career.

 **DON'T!** Dilute Your Efforts: Don't create multiple different talks, workshops or take on unrelated gigs like moderating. Stick to perfecting one exceptional talk. Diversifying too early will dilute your impact and hinder your progress.

 **DO!** Listen to Your Audience: Continuously improve your talk based on audience feedback. Adopt a Kaizen approach, making incremental, continuous improvements. Your audience's reactions are your best guide to what works and what doesn't. If you are a little bit ashamed of what you did a few years ago, it's a sign you have improved.

**DON'T!** Experiment Onstage:
Avoid trying new material
during paid engagements.
Keep your innovation and
experimentation for smaller,
less critical settings. Reliability
and consistency are key to
building a solid reputation.

 **DO!** Embrace the Process:
Understand that becoming
a great speaker is a journey.
Embrace the long road of
refinement and repetition.
Each performance is an
opportunity to polish your
diamond further.

 **DON'T!** Take Yourself Too Seriously:
Remember, you are not your
talk. Maintain humility and
perspective. The accolades
and compliments are for
your well-crafted product,
not your persona. Stay
grounded and focused on
continuous improvement.

# THE FOURTH
# COMMANDMENT

# THOU SHALT WORSHIP NO OTHER GODS THAN NUTRITIOUS TURDS

*Once your speaking career is up and running, 97% of all feedback you get will be – and should be – positive. People will call you awesome and want to shake your hand, take selfies and even sleep with you after you've closed with a mic drop at some event in Stockholm or San Francisco. You should ignore, decline or just politely respond to these requests. People prefer being positive and hanging out with people they think are successful. It is, in other words, not about you as a person. Sometimes, however, you'll get awful feedback. A katana-sharpened knife of a sentence designed to wound you and hack your carefully crafted speech to bits. Some of these comments will be correct. They will be turds but of the nutritious kind. Chew on them long and hard, as they are the only things that will make you better, whereas selfies or sleeping with others can only give you hubris and/or STDs.*

The Croatian sun shone on the taxi I was sitting in, and the Adriatic glistened outside the window. It was the first day of a family vacation. I had just flown in from delivering a talk in Denmark the day before.

My mind wandered in the back seat as the Dalmatian landscape sped by outside.

Things felt good.

It would not last.

A digital chime pierced the back-seat bliss, announcing the arrival of an email on my phone.

I opened it and could see from the amount of text that this would not be good.

It was regarding the Danish session and read as follows:

"Yesterday's session was a total disaster.

Firstly, as agreed in writing and on the phone, we did not get an in-depth introduction to key trends. We got some generic thinking that, at best, was inspiring but, on the other hand, not at all in alignment with our agreed focus.

Secondly, you ventured off into very normative advice on our strategy that was absolutely off and not based on any deeper insights. It is OK to suggest and give ideas – we love that – but mindlessly dictating what we should or should not do was inappropriate.

Thirdly, the Q&A session developed into a disastrous mocking and ridiculing of us – making inappropriate jokes about the top management team's looks, criticizing the mission statement, etc. I tried my best to signal and stop it – but you just went on and on. We are absolutely speechless and have never experienced a situation like this.

After the meeting, we needed to handle a furious team that felt really insulted. You stepped way over the line in every possible way. It was a real disaster.

Based on the above, we would like to claim the fee back, and we do not see ourselves in any position to pay for the services, as the agreed terms were violated. Further, we will discontinue our work with you now and in the future.

Sincerely
(NAME REDACTED)"

I was flabbergasted. I sat with my mouth agape as I read these words and felt tremors weld up inside of me. While I did not feel that the session was one of my better ones, calling it a disaster was not in my vocabulary. The client felt personally offended and even wounded.

By a talk? I thought it was the pen, not PowerPoint slides, that was mightier than the sword.

This would haunt me for many years. I underwent all phases – denial, vehement defence, anger and resignation – until I realized that it was a nutritious turd, something very uncomfortable that exists to make you better. This is a chapter about the kind of fuckups that make you wiser.

# DOUBLE-LOOP LEARNING IS THE ONLY LEARNING

A few weeks before the Denmark debacle, I received feedback from a German ventilation company after a speech: "What a mind-blowing performance by Magnus yesterday! Our employees were stunned and gave him a standing ovation. He brings such magnitude and force onto the stage that people hang on his lips, gestures and storyline. I have never experienced such a speech full of intelligent content and, at the same time, fabulous entertainment – to the point and all in one flow."

It was little consolation after being more or less decapitated by the Danish email. Yet the strange thing was that I had given the same speech in both instances. A self-help book or one of those self-aggrandizing motivational videos that thrive on social media would have latched on to the latter email and insinuated that the Danes were fools. The object of this chapter is the exact opposite; only the kind of feedback Denmark gave is useful. Having people tell you what a wonderful speaker you are will only make you complacent.

People prefer flattery and lies that lead them astray to honest truths that can put them right. What nutritional turds do is enable double-loop learning. If you've established yourself as a Mercedes S-Class speaker – reliable and reassuringly expensive – it is merely a qualifier, not a differentiation, that you get good feedback, just like we expect a Mercedes to be fast, comfortable and safe. Positive feedback enables no learning; only negative feedback does that. Double-loop learning happens when you are forced to analyse why something did not work and then change your approach accordingly. *Kaizen* – continuous improvement – happens only when you discover faults and flaws. The market will show you what works – you suggest, and the market rejects. Vehemently, in the Denmark case.

# THE HOLY GRAIL ...
# OF CUSTOMER
# FEEDBACK

Yet the market is not always right, because many stakeholders are involved when you deliver a talk. The person who booked you might have certain opinions, whereas the audience might have completely different ones. Remember the tenet of business as it applies to the speaking world: it may look like the audience is there for the magnificent You (capital Y). They are not. In professional speaking, they have likely not paid out of their pocket to see you.

Take the feedback I received after giving a speech at a project management conference in Rome:

> "Magnus certainly has a 'big' personality, and our attendees were very excited to hear from him. His book was sold out before his session began. Unfortunately, as a conference content professional working in this industry for many years, I was not pleased with his presentation delivery. While his overall message was

well received, Magnus, at times during
his presentation, chose to deliver the
message by cursing/swearing from
the stage (in one comment calling an
attendee a "crazy motherfucker") and
then calling out two ladies who were
getting up from their seats to leave
the session about 40 minutes into his
presentation. I am not clear if they left
because they were insulted or if they had
to catch their flight home. Also, by calling
these two ladies out from the stage, the
room of 400 attendees turned around to
look at them.

"The cursing did not stop, as words
were intermittently used throughout the
rest of the presentation. My manager,
whom Magnus met earlier, changed her
seat from the back of the room to the
front row in hopes of getting Magnus'
attention and being present, as our board
and management team was also sitting
up front.

"Concerning his physical slide presentation,
the PowerPoint that was emailed to
me in a PDF did not include all of the
slides presented in his Macbook keynote
presentation. Specifically, one slide
included a Michelangelo portrait of

THE BUSINESS OF SPEAKING

naked bodies. (Our congress audience is a mix of cultures, where this kind of artistry could be deemed offensive).

"Again, while the attendee feedback is mixed, I believe Magnus could have delivered his keynote presentation in a more professional manner so our attendees would have received the same message without the risk of being offended. Please note that when we reviewed Magnus' profile and past recordings, there was no indication that he would present in such a manner."

At first glance, this is very negative feedback, and one part of me wanted to apologize profusely while the other part wanted to tell them to go to, well, fuck off. However, the conference content professional was not the audience. The outcome of the speech in Rome was one of the highest referral rates I have ever had. I was booked to speak all over Europe, in the US, and in the United Arab Emirates, a conservative Muslim country, despite the perceived vulgarity of Michelangelo's art (when in Rome, it's probably rare that people are offended by the Sistine Chapel ceiling). In the speaking business, polarizing an audience can be lucrative.

A good talk needs to inspire, motivate and have people unanimously praise you. Good business only needs to get somebody somewhere to book you because they have heard you create something that makes waves. Just like the sign of having a strong brand is that some love while others hate you – think McDonald's – the sign of having a good speaking product is that it stirs up emotion in the audience.

# CONCLUSION: OWN IT!

As you progress in your speaking career, a hundred yeses will have to become many nos. What you learn by getting thrashed by feedback is what you should say yes and no to. You find your market fit.

In Denmark, I was booked by a third party – a management consultancy – whereas the people listening had very little experience of – or interest in – keynote speakers. They might even have mistaken me for being a management consultant, in which case their taking offense makes sense.

In Rome, the bookers were an American organization and, in the US, edginess plays less well on a broad level. American law even stipulates that it is unlawful to "utter any obscene, indecent or profane language by means of radio communication." When U2 won a Grammy award in 2003, the TV network had to pay a fine because Bono, with exuberant delight, said, "This is really fuckin' brilliant," live on air.

You don't have to decline requests from the US or Danish middlemen; you can adjust accordingly. Sometimes, that entails saying no altogether, and sometimes, you just remove some modules – cursing, for example – and add others to your McTalk.

Furthermore, you should take responsibility. We live in a world where we are often told to stand our ground and fight for what we believe in. If you're an activist or politician, that is probably good advice, but in business, the customer is always right, even when they are wrong.

Apologize, take responsibility, and adjust. Own your fuckups, in other words (sorry, American broadcasters).

Here is what I wrote to my Danish client once my emotions had subsided:

> "First of all, let me say that I am deeply sorry your client was unhappy and that my conduct in any way jeopardized your relationship with them. I take the accusation very seriously and it was not my intent – nor my grasp of the situation – that my presentation was delivered in an unprofessional, damaging manner.
>
> "Let me untangle what you wrote and give my reflections, which should not be perceived as belittling the apology above.

"I perceived the brief to be more general than what you specify here ('in-depth introduction to relevant trends'). I am fully conscious that procuring my services can be tricky given that you want a surprise element, a broader view and not just the usual suspects regarding trends. We covered several areas, but if you wanted a more in-depth view of that, I can see how you felt the material was 'generic thinking.'

"We did have quite a heated exchange that, at times, bordered on the accusatory on my part. I used the number of Rolex watches – and the fact that they were seven older men and one woman – to make a point that to be the 'most innovative company,' you must change who you are, not just how you work. Furthermore, I used their mission statement and criticized them for not seeming to use it, live it or even believe in it. Could I have wrapped this in different words? Of course! But I stand by my point that for your client to succeed in their ambition and goal, they – the leaders, their values and what they stand for – must change.

"Think about it: it is unlikely that the team
would have been offended if my comments
had been completely inaccurate.

"In conclusion, I do not share your
description of the session as a 'total
disaster,' but I fully respect your
viewpoint and apologize.

"It would, however, be deeply
disconcerting if the outcome of this
session is that I never get to work with
you again. I have loved being a virtual
member of the (name of consultancy
redacted) tribe and see each interaction
with you as a source of joy and learning."

Alas, I never heard from them again.

Thou shalt worship no other gods than nutritious turds.

Even when the turds sometimes win.

**DO!** Embrace Critical Feedback: Treat harsh criticism as valuable, nutritious turds. Analyse and learn from it to improve your craft. It's the uncomfortable truths that will push you to become a better speaker.

 **DON'T!** Seek Validation: Don't let positive feedback inflate your ego or distract you from areas needing improvement. Praise is comforting but often unhelpful for growth.

 **DO!** Engage in Double-Loop Learning: Use negative feedback to reassess and adjust your approach. Continuous improvement comes from understanding what didn't work and making necessary changes.

**DON'T!** Dismiss Harsh Criticism:
Avoid ignoring or brushing off
negative feedback, no matter
how painful it is to hear. These
insights are essential for your
development and future success.

 **DO!** Own Your Mistakes:
Take responsibility for your
missteps and address them
openly. Apologize when
necessary and demonstrate
a commitment to betterment.
This shows professionalism
and integrity.

 **DON'T!** Become Defensive:
Don't get defensive or
argumentative when faced
with negative feedback.
Accept it with grace and use
it constructively. Defensive
reactions hinder your ability to
learn and grow.

**DO!** Adjust Accordingly: Modify your approach based on the context and audience feedback. Be flexible and willing to change elements of your talk to better suit different settings and expectations.

 **DON'T!** Stick to a Single Approach: Avoid rigidly sticking to one style or content format. Be adaptable and ready to tweak your presentation as needed based on feedback and the specific audience.

**DO!** Focus on Improvement:
Continuously refine your talk,
aiming to turn every piece of
feedback into a stepping stone
toward excellence. Strive for a
consistent, high-quality delivery
every time.

 Get Complacent:
Don't rest on your laurels.
Even when feedback is
overwhelmingly positive,
there's always room for
improvement. Stay committed
to honing your craft.

THE FIFTH
COMMANDMENT

# THOU SHALT PRACTISE THE FINE ART OF R&D

*As in Rip Off and Duplicate. Consume a massive number of speeches and speakers. Sit through good and bad, high and low. Copy what works relentlessly. Jim Jarmusch said it well: "Nothing is original. Steal from anywhere that resonates with inspiration or fuels your imagination. Devour old films, new films, music, books, paintings, photographs, poems, dreams, random conversations, architecture, bridges, street signs, trees, clouds, bodies of water, light and shadows. Select only things to steal from that speak directly to your soul. If you do this, your work (and theft) will be authentic. Authenticity is invaluable; originality is nonexistent. And don't bother concealing your thievery – celebrate it if you feel like it. In any case, always remember what Jean-Luc Godard said: 'It's not where you take things from, it's where you take them to.'"*

Fifty hours of airplane travel is possibly the worst preparation you can have as a speaker. I had been booked on a speaking tour in the Far East and criss-crossed the skies between Singapore, Hong Kong, Kuala Lumpur and mainland China for over a week. I have a mild fear of flying, so the seasonal thunderstorms made every journey unpleasant. Furthermore, I had very little speaking experience in any of these countries – what worked, what did not – so every speech was like being an amateur again. When I say to do a hundred bad speeches, it only works in the specific context in which you gave them. You are back to square one if you change the locale or role. It was now time to give the final speech of the tour, and my brain and body were pummelled by jetlag, constant audience bewilderment and disappointment. I took to the stage and started going through the motions. Until suddenly, I couldn't. I stumbled on the word 'optimism' and had to repeat it slowly: 'op-ti-mi-sm.' My mind was blank. What should I say next? I repeated optimism again, drawing out the 'smmmm' even more, hoping it could break the spell I had obviously fallen under. To no avail. I tried saying the word quickly and abruptly. It made part of the audience chuckle. I said it even quicker three times in a row. The audience was laughing and clapping. I found my footing and could proceed. The speech got the best evaluations on the tour and many remarked how 'entertaining' and 'powerful' it was when I repeated the word 'optimism.' If they only knew what a moment of panic it had been for me.

It is a valuable lesson: giving a speech is make-believe, like special effects. It's about what works (and does not) onstage. In other words, find and use anything that works when you give a talk. It may include faking it, copying, stealing or being wholly insincere, even a liar. Drawing a complete blank and stumbling on a word qualifies too.

# HIT-OLOGY

The idea that there is a formula to create a hit single is offensive in artistic circles. In fact, one of the most damning adjectives about creation is that something is 'formulaic.' Had this been a book that treated speeches like a work of art, I, too, would have brought up the Greek masters of rhetoric, ground on and on about ethos, pathos and logos. This is akin to the musical principles and craftsmanship in a classical concert hall or opera house. They are indeed the foundation for music, and their artistic value is incalculable, but the commercial potential is often found wanting, which is why opera houses and concert halls are often grant- or state-supported while the Taylor Swift or Slipknot concerts in the local stadium are not. If you want to make money as a speaker, foundational principles of rhetoric are unimportant. Crafting a bankable speech matters; to do that, you need to use whatever works in the market.

This is a provocative idea. The common conception of public speaking is that it is about things dear to your heart, a fight for what you believe in and a tool for convincing others. That a speech should be hit-driven can feel as insulting as Ibiza DJs and the Spice Girls once were. It's cheating. It's shallow. It's wrong. It is also lucrative, which is why it is useful in this book.

If you want to craft a bankable speech, here are three things you must remember.

## CADENCE – HOW YOU SAY THINGS – IS MUCH MORE IMPORTANT THAN CONTENT.

The music industry calls it 'sampling' – borrowing rhythms, riffs and melodies from songs that work. M.I.A.'s *Paper Planes* used The Clash's *Straight to Hell* as a base to build from. *Bootylicious* by Destiny's Child repurposed Stevie Nicks's *The Edge of Seventeen* and ABBA permitted Madonna to use the melodic rhythm from *Gimme, Gimme, Gimme* in her smash hit *Hung Up*. If you want to make your speech a hit, sample from whatever works. Look at TED talks, political speeches, Oscar thank yous and the keynote speeches of your peers. Whenever you see or hear something that resonates with the audience – study their reaction closely – copy and paste it. In an age where information is abundant at your fingertips, extensive research has less value.

Everyone can say anything. How they say it makes all the difference.

A good talk should be only mildly useful, not an instruction manual.

## HUMOUR IS THE ULTIMATE MIND-OPENING TOOL.

One of the most damning comments about my talk was given by the CEO of one of the so-called Big Four accountancy firms. He called me a stand-up comedian and urged his peers to avoid listening to 'this clown.' His plea went unheeded. I'd had the audience in stitches, not because what I said was particularly funny but because I've learned – by giving a hundred bad talks and copying what works – that laughter is the sound of minds opening. When you say something slightly unexpected, even contrarian, the brain cannot help but respond with 'haha's.'

Ensuring that there is laughter at regular intervals from beginning to end in your talk means that people will like it – even if they cannot recite what the talk was about. The best feedback you can ever get is when people say, "I really like the talk!

I can't say what it was about, but it was really good." Think about it: if people could recite exactly what your talk was about, there would be no point in paying you to repeat it.

## IF THE SMARTEST PEOPLE IN THE ROOM LIKE YOUR TALK, EVERYONE WILL.

An audience works like a hierarchy where the smartest people are kings or queens. If they laugh at and enjoy your talk, the less gifted will not want to seem like they missed out and, therefore, nod along vigorously.

Too many speakers cater to the lowest common denominator, resulting in half the audience detesting your talk. If the smartest ten per cent like it, everyone will. So how do you do it? Easy. Make some points of your talk esoteric, even impossible to understand. Add many figures and charts, but be hazy, even opaque, when you describe them. I've given talks to management consultancies – infamous for the amount of competitive brainpower in the room – and removed every other slide to ensure that the talk made less sense. It worked every time

– the top ten per cent, who also found it
hard to keep up with what I was saying,
proclaimed their love and respect, and
the others followed along. You'll recognize
the ten per cent-ers by their position in
the room – at the very back – and body
language – crossed arms and constant
bored frown.

There is actually a fourth point to make here. But it's
so shallow that it doesn't deserve its own headline. It
is an alarmingly common mistake made by speakers.
Never, ever, wear black. You are there to be seen, not to
blend in with the scenery. Use colour; it doesn't matter
which, as long as it's not black. Black clothes are a sign
that, deep down, you really don't want to be there.

Wearing something mildly irritating is always a good
idea. If a couple of people in the audience really hate
you and the others love you, it is a sign that you're
doing a good job.

You will undoubtedly be offended by how blatantly
calculated these tips are. This is exactly the point: the
art of making music should not be mistaken for the art
of making money through hit singles. For the former,
skill and sincerity are key. For the latter, all you need is
to copy what already works.

# CONCLUSION:
# BE A DJ OF IDEAS!

I've seen Nobel laureates, renowned professors and intellectually brilliant scientists put entire audiences to sleep. Experts are needed to make decisions and formulate political policy but tend not to give particularly captivating talks. This is due to the so-called 'curse of knowledge' – they know so much that they often fail to grasp the limits of the audience's comprehension and interest. Something similar happens when native English speakers try to communicate with a non-English speaking audience and throw around British idioms like 'beat around the bush' or American sports metaphors.

Public speaking is the only profession where grifting is allowed, even encouraged. Not the criminal kind, intentionally seeking to mislead for the benefit of the grifter, but the kind where you can say things that are somewhat economical with the truth. A speech is more akin to storytelling than scientific discourse, hence the need to be selective about facts and choose only what can propel the narrative drive – the almighty cadence.

We will return to the ethical dilemmas of being a professional speaker in the final chapter of this book. There are several of them, but they are not unique to the speaking business, and many industries have significantly greater moral challenges to resolve.

Somebody once said an advertisement has three purposes: to be seen, to be heard and to be believed. Similarly, a good speaker gives the impression of being sincere. They talk as if they are great thinkers. They also persuade the audience that they are experts on their topic. But it's the make-believe that matters. It's the effect the talk has on the audience, not the underlying mechanisms or what is going on within the speaker.

Be a DJ of ideas. Sample the best beats, bass lines, hooks and riffs from wherever you find them.

Blend them. Let it stir.

Copy to uniqueness.

Thou shalt practise the fine art of Rip Off & Duplicate.

And yes, I stole this creative interpretation of 'R&D' from a seminar in Orlando in 2007.

**DO!** Rip Off and Duplicate: Actively seek out and study a wide range of speeches. Borrow elements that work well and incorporate them into your own presentations. Embrace the idea that originality is a myth and focus on creating an authentic mix of borrowed brilliance.

❌ **DON'T!** Obsess over Originality: Don't waste time trying to be entirely original. Authenticity comes from how you use what you've borrowed, not from creating something entirely new from scratch. Celebrate your influences openly.

 **DO!** Prioritize Cadence over Content: Focus on how you deliver your speech more than the content itself. Mimic successful rhythms, tones and pacing. Study TED talks, political speeches and award acceptance speeches to understand what makes audiences respond positively.

**DON'T!** Overvalue Detailed Research: Don't get bogged down in extensive research. Instead, prioritize elements that engage and entertain your audience. A good speech should be engaging and mildly informative, not an exhaustive instruction manual.

 **DO!** Use Humour to Open Minds: Integrate humour throughout your speech to keep the audience engaged and receptive. Aim for regular laughs to maintain attention and make your message memorable.

 **DON'T!** Cater to the Lowest Common Denominator: Avoid trying to please everyone with basic content. Target the top ten per cent of your audience with more complex ideas and let the rest follow their lead. This strategy ensures broader audience engagement.

**DO!** Wear Eye-Catching Colours: Choose clothing that stands out onstage. Avoid black and opt for colours that draw attention. Your appearance should reflect confidence and make you more visible to the audience.

 **DON'T!** Blend In:
Don't dress to fade into the background. Your presence onstage should be visually engaging. Wearing something mildly irritating can provoke strong reactions, which is better than being forgettable.

**DO!**    Be a DJ of Ideas:
Mix and match the best
elements from various sources
to create a compelling and
unique presentation. Blend your
influences seamlessly to form a
cohesive and engaging speech.

**DON'T!**  Ignore Audience Feedback:
Don't overlook the reactions
and feedback of your audience.
Use their responses to refine
and improve your speech.
Be adaptive and willing to
make changes based on
what resonates.

# THE SIXTH
# COMMANDMENT

# THOU SHALT TREAT OTHER SPEAKERS WITH GRACE AND GENEROSITY

*Other speakers only look like competitors, because there is no such thing as competition in public speaking. If you do a good job with a client this year, they will want somebody else equally good next year. If some speakers are booked for the same day and conference, the best thing that can happen is that they are all stellar. A dozen speakers will then be booked for next year's event. You should, in other words, be courteous and generous with other speakers. Help them, love them and ask them how they're doing. Don't fidget with a smartphone when you listen to them. Recommend them to clients. Woe to you if anything like a snide remark or criticism finds its way onto any social media platform.*

I realized that something was off when the moderator
called my name as a cue to walk onstage. There was no
polite applause, just a loud murmur, as if the audience
was confused. At least the other speakers entered to
the sound of hands clapping. And surely, I was a lot
better than they were.

Or so I thought.

The event was 'The Great Day of Inspiration' in Gothenburg's largest conference venue. Hundreds of people
had paid – or had their company pay – to attend a
packed agenda full of "leadership advice, inspirational
stories and thought leadership."

Mountain climbers, stand-up comedians and management gurus were to share the eight-hour agenda and
give the audience value for their money.

The big draw was supposed to be the late, great Professor Hans Rosling of TED Talk fame. He had garnered
a reputation in Sweden as a straight-talking, no-non-
sense public health professor invited to news broad-
casts and talk shows to share his unorthodox view of
health, Africa, pandemics and beyond. He had reached
nearly god-like status at this time, and most of the
audience was there solely for him.

Only, he had cancelled due to ill health, and I would be his replacement. It was a daunting task, but I felt ready, willing and able to step out of his shadow and into the limelight.

All the other speakers that day had been underwhelming, or so I thought. Mediocre amateurs and nowhere near the prestigious speaking slot given to me, the Great Futurologist.

I waited anxiously in the wings for my chance to shine. Outshine the others and let the audience know that I was the Crown Prince to Rosling's King.

If only the organizers had told the audience in advance that there would be no Rosling.

As the moderator started to announce the next speaker, you could hear the disappointment rising from the crowd. No applause for me, just a bewildered murmur with a palpable sense of irritation. They had all been tricked, so they wouldn't cancel their tickets.

Instead of a beloved deity, some random dude stood onstage before them.

To them, I was not even a nobody but less than zero.

Whatever I tried in my talk, nothing worked. Not humour, not inspiration, not a single one of my examples.

I might have managed the odd giggle or lazy hand clap as I walked off stage, but I doubt it.

On a day full of mediocre amateurs, I became the worst-rated speaker. And I deserved it. This chapter is about keeping your head out of what I call 'the asshole sky' and staying grounded, curious and courteous, especially when it comes to dealing with other speakers.

# THE CHAMPIONSHIP
# VOID

Sigmund Freud, the renowned psychologist, high-lighted a peculiar aspect of human behaviour: our tendency to engage in conflict, ridicule or argument stems more from a hyperawareness of minor differences among us than from significant disparities. This phenomenon, strikingly evident in the intense rivalries between football teams from the same city, is what Freud termed the 'narcissism of small differences.' This same concept applies to the speaking community, particularly evident during events like 'The Great Day of Inspiration.' Despite speakers sharing professions, platforms and the goal to inspire, these similarities can paradoxically fuel feelings of animosity among them.

The speaking profession isn't immune to other, broader social phenomena either. 'Tall Poppy Syndrome' in Australia describes the critique and envy directed at those who have achieved success, particularly if that success is seen as unearned. This sentiment is not unique to any one culture; it finds echoes in the Japanese proverb, "The nail that sticks up gets hammered down," and the Nordic Law of Jante, "You're not to think you are anything special," among others. These societal attitudes, often dismissed as mere jealousy, play a crucial role. They remind us that success is not solely the result of individual effort but also involves a significant degree of luck. This is particularly relevant in public speaking, a field with low entry barriers and no clear parameters for competition, leading to what we can call the 'championship void.'

This void can foster resentment and paranoia as speakers obsessively compare income statements, social media engagement and audience feedback to gauge their relative standing. The lack of a clear 'winner' or 'loser,' as found in sports competitions, exacerbates this issue. However, during the conference in Gothenburg, I realized that this perspective is fundamentally flawed. Unlike in competitive sports, success in speaking is not zero-sum. A well-received presentation benefits the speaker *and* enhances the event's overall value, encouraging audiences to return. The real adversary is not other speakers, but events that fail to offer professional, engaging presentations, leaving audiences to endure lacklustre speeches or workshops. In truth, we are all in this together, striving to create memorable and enriching experiences for our listeners.

# IT'S LONELY
# AT THE TOP AND
# THE BOTTOM

There are few professions as lonely as public speaking. You travel alone, sit alone, are invited to events as an outsider and perform on a stage in isolation. To keep your sanity in check requires a careful balancing act between stimulation – without overdoing it with substance abuse or gambling addiction – and boredom. The hours take their toll, and if you are far away from loved ones and feel the effects of sleep deprivation, self-hatred can easily set in. It happens to most speakers – and most people – at some point.

When I spoke at an event called Change Makers Lab – a day focusing on sustainability and the circular economy – it happened to a fellow speaker of mine, who could not refrain from writing the following about my talk: "In the future, futurologists will hopefully have fewer quotes, fewer funny images and fewer ppts. #changemakerslab." It was a comment intended to mock and ridicule. Even though my name was not mentioned, my job title and the event name made it easy to see whom the comment targeted. I felt wounded, of course, but I knew the comments came from a place of hurt and despair – as if the attention I got onstage was stolen from him. I, too, have made similar comments and know they are the bastard children of resentment, envy and loneliness. The corrosive effects of being a public speaker take their toll in the long run, and nobody is immune to it. This is why the profession owes itself compassion, camaraderie and tips for resilience.

Digital etiquette – being kind, encouraging and courteous – goes without saying, but it must be taken further. Be candid about your failures and shortcomings, as they will help others see the pitfalls. Be open about mental suffering, as it makes you relatable. Be kind to yourself and others – the only known antidote to loneliness. And always, always push the elevator back down again.

# CONCLUSION: ABOVE ALL, BE CHARMING!

The seventh tenet of business stated: "It's better to be charming than not. People prefer doing business with pleasant people rather than assholes." When you are affected by Tall Poppy Syndrome, the narcissism of small differences, and grasping at straws in the championship void, this is easily forgotten. You slowly become a resentful, jealous and bitter lone wolf, not the eager person you once were. To have any kind of longevity in a career, you must fight this transformation. Some actors like Stellan Skarsgård, Helen Mirren and Michael Caine have worked in Hollywood for decades, while more talented stars are long forgotten. The secret is that the actors with long careers are charming. They talk to everyone. They bring gifts or cook food. They don't hide away in a trailer but spend time on set to interact with the cast and crew.

Make it about them, not about you.

When you have established yourself on the speaker circuit, you must leave your ego out of the equation. Your name may be on the invitation and people might even have paid money to see you but it's nothing personal, they are there to be entertained – or should that be 'infotained' – and you are of no greater importance than the supplier of the lights, projectors or coffee and sandwiches during the break.

Be the person who others like having around.

Thou shalt treat other speakers – and everybody else – with grace and generosity.

**DO!** Support Fellow Speakers: Actively help and encourage other speakers. Share advice, recommend them to clients and celebrate their successes. A rising tide lifts all boats, and a community of excellent speakers benefits everyone.

 **DON'T!** See Them as Competition: Don't view other speakers as rivals. The speaking circuit thrives on variety and excellence, and one speaker's success doesn't detract from another's. Avoid jealousy and rivalry.

 **DO!** Listen Attentively: Pay full attention when other speakers are presenting. Put away your smartphone, engage with their content and show genuine interest. Your respect and attention matter.

**DON'T!** Criticize Publicly:
Avoid making snide remarks
or negative comments about
other speakers on social media
or in public. Maintain a positive
and supportive demeanour,
both online and offline.

 **DO!** Offer Constructive Feedback:
When appropriate, provide
thoughtful and constructive
feedback to fellow speakers.
Focus on helping them improve
and grow, rather than tearing
them down.

 **DON'T!** Undermine Others:
Don't undermine or belittle
other speakers to make
yourself look better. Success
in public speaking is not a
zero-sum game, and lifting
others up creates a better
environment for all.

**DO!** Stay Humble:
Remember that your role as a
speaker is to serve the audience,
not to feed your ego. Keep
your feet on the ground, stay
approachable and maintain
humility no matter how
successful you become.

 **DON'T!** Succumb to Jealousy:
Resist the urge to compare
yourself to others or feel envious
of their success. Focus on your
own growth and development
and celebrate the achievements
of your peers.

**DO!**    Promote Camaraderie:
Foster a sense of community
among speakers. Share your
experiences, challenges and
victories. Building strong,
supportive relationships will
enrich your career and
personal life.

  Isolate Yourself:
Avoid becoming a lone wolf in
the speaking industry. Isolation
can lead to resentment and
negativity. Engage with others,
build connections and be part
of the speaker community.

# THE SEVENTH COMMANDMENT

# THOU SHALT TREAT MIDDLEMEN LIKE INSECTS

*Insects are annoying, but they underpin the whole ecosystem. Don't swat them away – be grateful that they do what you will not or cannot. Always let speaker agents and events people get the last percentage point and final say. An executive assistant at a large company based in Brussels or Bangalore rarely reaches out directly to a speaker but always asks speaker agencies to recommend four or five names suitable for their planned event. Make sure you're one of these four or five people because you're kind, generous and easy to work with in the eyes of the speaker agency.*

The lunch cost me nearly 10,000 euros. It was worth it.

The occasion was neither a birthday nor an anniversary. It was the annual Christmas lunch for a renowned speaker agency, and I was paying for it.

They were worth it. They had given me dozens of assignments over the course of a year and even chosen to give me their coveted 'Speaker of the Year' award. It was not given out for excellence in speaking – though many clients thought so – but rather something given to speakers who were easy to work with. The kind of people who said yes to anything and everything. Although my bio described me as a futurologist who spoke on trends and the future, they had sent me on assignments to talk about coping with change in front of hundreds of ambulance drivers and a national gathering of judges who just wanted "something fun and different." I had become their 'duct-tape' speaker, a one-solution answer to whatever challenge or problem their clients had thrown at them. It had been somewhat lucrative for me. It had been very lucrative for them. So, of course, it was only right that I bankroll their Christmas lunch.

Although it may seem like the speaker industry is made up of charismatic speaker stars with important messages – just like the music industry minus, well, music – in reality, it's made up of overstretched assistants and event managers who turn to speaker agencies for peace of mind. To them, the speakers are commodities and afterthoughts.

This chapter is about the many layers of people who stand between you and an audience in the speaker profession – the insects that will continuously pollinate your career.

# THE ECOSYSTEM

## CLIENTS

To put it bluntly, you will never know where clients come from and what they will pay. When you're green and starting out, the idea that someone will pay you tens of thousands to come and 'infotain' them seems outlandish. If you stick to it, money will flow from the most unexpected places. An accountancy summit in Lahore. Gym owners in Texas. Six bored men in a wine cellar in Manchester (an actual speaking engagement I did) and so on. The point is that it is hard to generalize about who clients are and what they want, but to make an attempt, it is good to think about what planning horizon they have and what size the event is. A last-minute booking for a boardroom meeting will be happy with almost anything (unless the client is Danish, obviously), whereas a congress booking you a year in advance will want several conference calls to follow up, make sure you understand their brief, share opinions about whatever you suggest as a title and contents.

I've found that clients are either high-trust ("Do something cool for us – no need to check with us in advance") or no-trust ("Please send over a two-page synopsis before our committee meeting where every comma, punctuation mark and word choice will be dabbled over."). When they decide whether to book you or not, they might ask the dreaded question: "How many talks do you give per year?" This is dreaded because they will want one of two mutually exclusive answers, and you will be forced to lie to get the deal. The high-trust client looking for something unique will ideally want you to answer something like, "Not many; actually, I spend most of my time on research, writing books and exploring interesting ideas." The no-trust client prefers that you reply, "Nearly a hundred, and I feel very comfortable with the brief you have given me."

Clients seek peace of mind, but your way of putting them at ease will differ.

Speaking of clients, the big and global ones tend not to pay small suppliers on time, which brings us to the speaker agencies.

## SPEAKER AGENCIES

To repeat business tenets four and five: "It is useless to be good at something if *you* cannot sell it, and if you cannot sell it, find somebody who can." Speaking agencies – when they are good – are selling machines, so they are particularly helpful when you reach for escape velocity before you make a name for yourself on the circuit. And afterwards, too. American clients tend to have endless bureaucratic exercises if you want to do business with them ("Does your one-person company have a 'diversity, equity and inclusion' plan in place?"). Speaking agencies help you with that. Banks in many countries have tightened rules around money transfers. Speaking agencies can help. Sometimes, some clients pay well, but you may not want to deal directly with them for publicity reasons – political parties, public sectors whose accounts are transparent to the general public or ethically challenged industries like gambling or tobacco. A speaking agency as a middleman solves this for you.

All you need to do is deliberately sacrifice profits: the agency takes around 30% or more. It is, in general, worth the sacrifice. They provide invaluable – if sometimes invisible – services to the speakers and clients alike.

To change the perspective to the client side, an agency is the gateway to the chaotic world of speakers. It is useful to remind yourself about the following: few people can name more than a handful of speakers, and they are bound to be the kind of global superstars – Simon Sinek or Brené Brown – who are very expensive and more than likely fully booked. Trying to search online for speakers is about as effective as googling to find good restaurants; the top results will all be sponsored links. Finding a fit for your event and needs is impossible if you try doing it alone. You will either fall back on referrals – what you or your colleagues have seen at other events – or require the help of a middleman to point the way.

And yes, speaker agencies will write up contracts and hunt down missing payments. Sacrificing 30% of a fee is better than not getting paid at all.

People who work at speaker agencies tend to be young, outgoing, social and eager to hear "Yes, no problem" from speakers and clients alike. Make friends with them early in your career. Send their office a crate of beer or wine once per year. Always give them the upper hand, the final say or the extra percentage point when negotiating. If you do, you become their go-to speaker they throw at anything, and you will rack up the proverbial 10,000 hours in no time.

## MANAGERS

Once escape velocity has been reached, sales and referrals take care of themselves, and it's time to transition from a hundred yeses to many nos; you will also need somebody to do what you cannot or should not do. If you're a yes-person, have somebody who can say no on your team. I used to accept speaking assignments all days of the week, sometimes for very little pay, to the detriment of marriage, wallet and mental health alike.

Furthermore, you will need a hand-on-the-shoulder person, somebody who can pull you back from getting agitated and,

like a Roman slave, remind you of your
own mortality. Being easy to work with is a
virtue that ensures longevity in the speaker
world, but when you have your head in the
asshole sky, it is easy to become a diva.

Managers tend to be one-person
operations managing one or a few
speakers. Some people work with their
spouse as their manager – don't! Working
with your spouse in any profession is a bad
idea. Marriage works as an equation: L+T-
D=H (love plus time minus distance equals
hate.) Do not socialize or make friends with
your manager. Do not entrust them with all
your banking details or innermost secrets.
Use them to do what you can't or won't do
on the speaking circuit. In my case, it was
saying no in a way that kept the client or
speaker agency on good terms.

## MICHAEL COLLINS

Most people know Neil Armstrong and
Buzz Aldrin. Few realize that perhaps
the most important man on that mission
was Michael Collins, who piloted the
spacecraft on the Apollo 11 mission. In
other words, he was the one who ensured
Armstrong and Aldrin could get to and

from the moon. The invisible yet vital component of the team.

Speaking is a lonely endeavour, and you will need a Michael Collins on your side: somebody who can help you get better at what you do over the long run. This might be a coach who can help you chisel out your message better, or it could be a friend with whom you can share your deepest, darkest fears. And with all these hours alone on planes and trains, trust me that there will be many dark thoughts that cross your mind.

# CONCLUSION: IF YOU WANT TO GO FAR, GO TOGETHER

Just like a supermarket is not a meritocracy, where all goods are displayed in an objective measurement of flavour and price, the speaker market is a manifestation of power and hidden relationships. Most speakers will get a chance to prove their worth once, but to stay in the game long term, you must cultivate relationships in the ecosystem described in this chapter. As this book progresses, it becomes increasingly clear that having a long-term career is about striking a balance. You must find ways to make the profession sustainable for you and others. What's the right mindset? What's the right ratio of yes to no? What do others need? What do you need? The next chapter will focus on what really matters in the business of speaking: the almighty dollar, euro or Swedish krona.

Thou shalt treat middlemen like insects. Their services are invaluable in the speaker ecosystem.

**DO!**     Cultivate Relationships
with Speaker Agencies:
Build strong, positive
relationships with speaker
agencies. Be generous, easy
to work with and willing to
accommodate their needs. They
are the gatekeepers to many
speaking opportunities.

 **DON'T!**   Swat Them Away:
Don't dismiss or undervalue the
role of speaker agencies and
event organizers. Their work is
essential in connecting you with
clients and managing logistics.

 **DO!**     Be Gracious and Appreciative:
Show appreciation for the work
that speaker agencies and event
managers do. Small gestures like
sending a crate of beer or wine
to their office can go a long way
in fostering goodwill.

**DON'T!** Be Difficult to Work With:
Avoid being demanding or
inflexible. Being easy to work
with will make agencies more
likely to recommend you for
future gigs.

 **DO!** Give Them the Upper Hand:
Always allow speaker agencies
to have the final say and
the last percentage point in
negotiations. This will ensure
they see you as a reliable and
cooperative partner.

 **DON'T!** Undermine Their Authority:
Don't try to bypass agencies or
undermine their role. Respect
their position in the ecosystem
and work within the frameworks
they establish.

 **DO!** Use Managers Wisely:
Hire a manager to handle
tasks you can't or shouldn't
do, such as saying no or
negotiating terms. Ensure they
are professional and maintain a
healthy working relationship.

**DON'T!** Mix Personal and Professional: Avoid working with close friends or family as your manager. Keep the relationship professional to prevent conflicts of interest and maintain clear boundaries.

 **DO!** Find Your Michael Collins: Identify and work with a supportive partner or coach who can help you improve and manage the stresses of a speaking career. Their support is crucial for long-term success.

 **DON'T!** Ignore the Ecosystem: Recognize that success in speaking involves navigating a complex ecosystem of clients, agencies, managers and other stakeholders. Build and maintain strong relationships across this network.

# THE EIGHTH
# COMMANDMENT

# THOU SHALT ONLY VALUE THE ALMIGHTY DOLLAR, EURO OR POUND

*Compliments, favours, prestige and book deals are nice things, but the only thing that will give you any kind of longevity in the speaker world is speaker fees. Get paid. No matter how little. Don't do favours. Don't do things that don't pay. Don't fall for flattery or awards. Just get paid. And raise your fee as your quality improves. Please note: €1,000 plus travel expenses is zero. You should decline anything below €5,000 unless you can defend it under the Second Commandment. A decent speaker commands between €10,000–15,000 in Europe and double that outside ... plus business class expenses. Make them pay if you have to spend time away from home and loved ones.*

It was evident from the lack of notes taken that the interview was a flop. The journalist had set aside an hour to get inspiration about emerging trends. Still, after 30 minutes, he wrapped up seemingly without getting anything remotely useful for the article he was writing. I was hungry for attention, so it was not without a slight sense of failure that I shook his hand and bid *adieu*. As we shook hands, he caught a glimpse of the yard in front of the office building where I was renting a small room. Scattered across the yard were vast mounds made out of thick glass that functioned as skylights for the basement underneath them. "They're really cool," he remarked and said that he would send a photographer over, and maybe I could pose by sitting atop one of them "for future reference" (i.e., in case they ever write something about me in the future and need a picture). The next day, a very ambitious young photographer arrived. She had been in touch with the building's caretaker and gained access to the space beneath the glass mounds to light them from within. It was a cold January day in Stockholm, so when she asked me to sit Buddha-like atop the mound, I assumed it would all be over in a minute or so. Nearly 40 minutes later, she was still snapping shots while my limbs were frozen and my face had numbed into a frown.

She left, and over the next couple of days, I forgot about the failed interview.

Then I got an email from the journalist who said that the editor had been so impressed with the photos that they wanted this to become the cover story.

"Problem is," giggled the journalist, "I don't have enough material for a cover story. And," he sheepishly added, "I'm going on a weekend trip with the missus." So, he inquired if I could write part of the article myself if he sent over a questionnaire.

This was Sweden's biggest business weekly magazine at the time, and landing on its cover was coveted among the business elite. I had been dealt a winning lottery ticket, in other words. Writing, in essence, my self-penned advertorial insert.

When the magazine was published a week later, I erupted onto the national stage of who's who. From feeling like a nobody delivering PowerPoint speeches, I became a somebody. Invitations to important events and parties started filling my inbox. Sponsorship deals were presented. I even had a restaurant offering me to eat and drink for free every day of the week as long as I showed up on their premises somewhat regularly.

I was invited to speak at Brilliant Minds, an invitation-only VIP event in Stockholm that makes Davos seem stale and unglamorous.

I had a very busy six months.

Then it hit me.

You cannot eat prestige.

The siren song had lured me away from my carefully crafted keynote speech and crash-landed me on the rocks of some arid island where the jaws of the Fame Monster were chewing on my time and self-respect.

It taught me the two most valuable pieces of advice if you want to do business as a public speaker: Get paid. Reject fame.

# WHAT IS MONEY?

Deeply dysfunctional societies – think failed states – usually rely on the family to get everything done. Instead of capitalism, they have vows, promises, loyalty and multigenerational memory. Justice tends to be done by *omertà* – blood libel. Trust is limited to people with the same last name or tribe affiliation.

In contrast, free societies tend to solve things with money. I pay you, so you don't have to owe me anything, and vice versa. Trust can be crafted with anyone who agrees to sign a contract. Money is the universal tool for negotiating and exchanging goods/services and signals what is worth a lot and what is worthless. True, there will come a day when this system has been replaced by something even better – bitcoin, blockchain, space sea shells, whatever – but for now, it is the best we have to get people to do something. Yet, for some peculiar reason, the speaking industry has a strange relationship with money. Many conferences refuse to pay speakers – TED, Brilliant Minds, World Economic Forum – while others charge money for people to speak on their stage

– IT conferences, industry congresses, etc. You often end up with a pile of stinking garbage onstage instead of a bona fide, professional speaker. I have sat through countless panels, interviews and infomercials in disguise. Time I will never get back.

This is why the most basic – and important – advice in a book about the business of speaking is to get paid. Do not speak at events that do not charge a fee.[4]

---

4   The exception is academia, charities and helping out a friend.

# WHAT'S THE PRICE?

There are two ways of crafting a price: one is to consider all the components and time involved in making the product and then add a markup.

The other – and more applicable method for speakers – is value pricing. Charge what the market thinks something is worth.

There is a famous anecdote about Picasso dining at a restaurant, and when the owner asked him to doodle on a napkin instead of paying the bill, Picasso replied: "I want to pay the bill, not buy the restaurant."

Becoming Picasso had taken many decades, even if a napkin doodle would only take a few seconds. Once you, as a speaker, have gone through the baptism by fuckups, you, too, can charge a lot of money for your services.

So, what is a lot of money? The sums mentioned in the opening of this chapter will, of course, vary greatly, but here are some useful tips:

- Be reassuringly expensive: Price is signalling. In
  mass markets, there are ways of selling things
  cheaply. IKEA can sell cheap furniture because it
  manufactures in low-cost countries and has the
  customers assemble everything themselves, often
  involving frequent swearing. A public speaker
  cannot work this way. You are more like a bottle
  of fine wine that has been distilled to perfection
  over the years and travelled far and wide to be
  with this particular audience today. The feeling
  you will give them is unique. Charge accordingly.

- Only about a third of potential clients should
  say yes once they learn what you charge. You are
  short selling yourself if everyone books you when
  you state your fee. Remember that the direct and
  indirect costs of organizing events easily run into
  hundreds of thousands of euros; your fee level
  should be high to signal that you are a sure thing.
  Many clients will say no to you because you are
  too expensive. This also frees time to think, write
  and hang out with family. In the future, the only
  people who will remember that you worked a lot
  are your children. Nobody will thank you for it.

- Lowering your price is not a sustainable strategy.
  Being self-employed is riddled with unease,
  uncertainty and monetary anxiety. It is often
  tempting to lower the price so that more clients
  will book you. This is akin to peeing your pants
  in the wintertime. A momentary relief will bring

discomfort in the long run. You cannot raise your price because you have signalled your willingness to sell yourself cheaply. One does not become a Mercedes by being a Skoda for a very long time. Furthermore, being busy might bring some mental relief, but you will sacrifice a priceless asset called freedom. Never compete on price.

# CONCLUSION: FAME IS CURRENCY ... AND DISTRACTION

Just because you cannot eat it does not mean fame is worthless. Quite the opposite. It is a currency. It will unlock doors, get you invitations and ensure that people will listen to you ... once, at least. It is also a time thief and a distraction. Every moment spent on a red carpet or in the audience at some event are moments you could have spent doing other things. And since fame is just a set of misunderstandings surrounding a new name, as somebody aptly pointed out, your fame will wane, and some new, hot thing will take your place. Focus on hovering slightly below the radar instead and get paid. Money is frozen freedom. If you save it, you can be in control of your destiny in a way you never can as the Fame Monster's slave.

And you should save it. Success does not last. All rich people spend little. I've spent too much.

Furthermore, hype and fame will distract you and prevent you from following this book's final commandment: Do what you are expected to do as a paid professional speaker – show up and do the work.

Thou shalt only value the almighty dollar, euro or pound.

**DO!** Value Your Time and Expertise:
Always charge a fee for your
speaking engagements. Ensure
your fee reflects the quality and
uniqueness of your presentation.
The only way to achieve
longevity in the speaking world
is by getting paid for your work.

 **DON'T!** Fall for Flattery or Favours:
Avoid doing engagements
for exposure, prestige or
compliments. These won't
pay your bills or secure your
future. Only accept speaking
opportunities that compensate
you fairly.

 **DO!** Set a Minimum Fee Threshold:
Establish a baseline fee that you
won't go below. For example,
€5,000 is a reasonable starting
point for a decent speaker in
Europe. Increase this fee as your
reputation and quality improve.

**DON'T!** Undervalue Yourself:
Don't accept low-paying gigs
or undervalue your services.
Doing so sets a precedent
that can be hard to break and
undermines your perceived
value in the market.

 **DO!** Raise Your Fees over Time:
As you gain experience and improve
your speaking quality, progressively
increase your fees. This signals
to clients that you're a premium
speaker worth the investment.

 **DON'T!** Lower Your Price Easily:
Resist the temptation to lower
your fees just to get more
bookings. This is a short-term
solution that will harm your
long-term value and reputation.

 **DO!** Ensure All Expenses Are Covered:
Make sure your speaking fee
includes travel expenses, ideally
business class if the event is
outside your home country. Your
time and comfort are valuable.

**DON'T!** Work for Free:
Avoid unpaid engagements
unless they fall under specific,
strategic exceptions. Free work
often leads to more free work,
not paid opportunities.

 **DO!** Treat Fame as a Tool,
Not a Goal:
Use any fame or recognition
you gain as a means to
command higher fees and
open doors to better-paying
opportunities. Keep your focus
on getting paid rather than
seeking fame for its own sake.

 **DON'T!** Get Distracted by Fame:
Don't let the allure of fame
distract you from your primary
goal: earning money through
speaking engagements.
Fame is fleeting and can
divert your attention from
what truly matters.

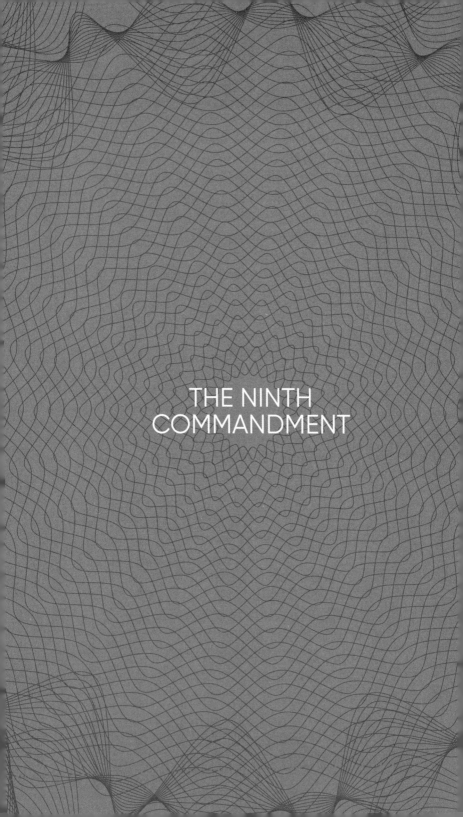

# THE NINTH
# COMMANDMENT

# THOU SHALT UNDERSTAND THAT NOT ALL SPEAKING ENGAGEMENTS ARE CREATED EQUAL

*The problem with money is that you can't see where it's from. Or how somebody got it. A million gained from a robbery looks and smells the same as a million made from a patent saving the lives of millions. Therefore, it should follow that a well-paid engagement in Singapore is equal to a well-paid engagement in San Francisco or Stockholm. Nothing could be further from the truth. While the pay may indeed be equal, there are places you will go that will embrace you, your message and invite you back to even more well-paid engagements. But there are places where the opposite is true. You'll be alone, superfluous in the agenda and nobody will remember that you were ever there. Except for the loved ones you left behind on your travels. The way to build your reputation and maintain your sanity is to be vigilant about WHERE in the world you speak.*

It was a warm September day in Stockholm. My twin boys, aged three at the time, were splashing around in an inflatable pool in our small garden. Birds were chirping in the trees. My wife was relaxing with a cup of coffee in a recliner next to the children. Autumn had not yet taken hold of Sweden.

It was a blissful image.

That I would have to leave behind.

I had been invited to speak at an agricultural conference in Bali on the other side of the world. While Balinese beaches strike many people as the very definition of a dream destination, I had a nightmare trip ahead of me. I was to fly from Stockholm via Bangkok to Bali. Spend less than 24 hours there. Then fly back to Sweden, not to go home but to speak in Gothenburg. From there, I would fly via Amsterdam to Atlanta to speak at Coca-Cola and leave within 12 hours to fly via Chicago to Brussels. All in all, I would be on the road for six days. Then, I would get to speak at an event at home before an equally nightmarish trip would ensue, taking me to Bristol in the UK, Newark in New Jersey and Helsinki, Finland. The only thing these two weeks had going for them was that they were very lucrative. But the money came at the expense of parenthood, relationships and peace of mind. More importantly, most of the engagements did not go particularly well. I showed up, delivered a keynote speech, got some applause and answered some questions. But – and I have double-checked this at the time of writing – not a single one of the engagements led to a referral. I had done a good job but merely being good does not referrals bring. For people to recommend you to other clients, you must have done a great job.

This chapter will explore how the *where* is the key to higher fees and longer careers.

# 'WHERE' BUILDS ...
# OR DESTROYS

What can you, as a speaker, learn from motorbike manufacturer Harley Davidson's perfume fiasco, Korean technology pioneer Samsung's pivot from low-price to high-end products, and luxury brand Gucci's return from a near-death experience? All three of them are about the power of distribution – the where – to wreck or boost a brand. Harley Davidson is legendary for their noisy, retro-styled and expensive motorcycles. When they decided to launch a perfume through a joint venture in the 1990s, it could have been a modest success. An investment banker paying hundreds of thousands for a new bike would easily have paid a few hundred for a bottle of perfume, like a cool reminder that he was part of a new tribe. But the perfume was not sold at a high price in the showrooms together with the bikes. They were sold in mass-market outlets like supermarkets and department stores. At a relatively modest price and in a cheap-looking bottle. The perfume is viewed as one of the greatest marketing failures in history. The 'where' wrecked Harley Davidson's lifestyle brand extension.

Samsung was selling cheap, inferior products for decades when, in the mid-1990s, their notorious Chairman Lee arranged a giant bonfire outside the factory and torched all the rubbish Samsung phones that the staff had received as a Christmas present. This historical moment marks the beginning of Samsung as a brand known for its design and innovation prowess. Yet there is another more important ingredient in their strategic shift: they decided to stop competing with cheap stuff in emerging markets and instead went into the most sophisticated and highly competitive places around the world, from the US and Europe to Japan. The 'where' forced them to work harder and be better as it removed the advantage you have when selling cheap stuff in Kenya or Kazakhstan – the option to make trade-offs in terms of design, innovation and, sometimes, quality.

Finally, while Gucci is today known as one of the most prestigious and luxurious haute couture brands in the world, they were a laughing stock in the 1970s and early 80s. They had overextended the brand, slapping the Gucci on everything from keyrings to wallets, and sold in all kinds of shops and stores. Luxury demands a sense of the unattainable; something cheap key rings has a hard time communicating. It was only when new management and the design genius Tom Ford took over in the 1990s that the fortune of Gucci was reversed, the brand rebuilt, and its stature reasserted. The key was to say no. To go from hundreds of meaningless products sold in all kinds

of channels, to a select few collections sold only in
bespoke Gucci stores.

Doing business is not just selling a bunch of things
to whomever, wherever. Strategy requires you to turn
down opportunities and craft a narrow target, even
if and especially when it requires of you to say no
to revenue.

# THE LEAKING
# BARREL

Imagine your brand as a speaker – your reputation for being very good at what you do – as a barrel full of water. The water is the value you have carefully built up over the years of delivering excellence. Now, this barrel is always leaking. There is a hole in the bottom that comes from brand erosion. Being on the circuit, repeating your speech over and over, and growing older take their toll and ensure that over time, what was once fresh, new and interesting is now a bit stale and unremarkable. It's the nature of markets over time and speakers are no exception. Apple's iPhone X was once the epiphany of cool. Now, you'd have a hard time finding anyone willing to pay money for it. That's why you constantly have to refill the barrel with new water to maintain brand value. Apple is known for launching new products and gadgets on a regular basis for that exact purpose. You, too, must ensure that you speak at the right events in the right places. If all you do is deliver content in second-tier cities in your home country, the barrel will dry up, together with your business, soon enough. Travelling from Ghent in Belgium to Wichita,

Kansas may feel exotic and the income from the two events may be great but they will do your reputation no favours. It is a bitter pill to swallow but unless most of the events you speak at are in major cities, you are probably not a very good speaker. You are the Gorenje, not the Miele or Whirlpool, of washing machines. Similarly, if you only speak in your home country, you've crafted something akin to the Tata Nano Car, sold only in India, not the Mercedes S-Class you need to become.

When I went from Bali to Helsinki, I was only raking in speaker fees, which was profitable in the short run. But I could – and should – have done without Indonesia and Finland. There is nothing wrong with them as countries. They are lovely to visit. But you are not a tourist when you travel for speaking work – you are logistically moving your body that, in turn, holds up your brain, mouth and vocal cords. Indonesia, Finland and Belgium are nobody's idea of global business hubs or brand-building platforms for business speakers. Not all places are created equal. To continuously boost your brand, ensure that you have a good number of prestigious events in prime locations so that your reputation can withstand a congress in Jyväskylä (third-tier town smack dab in the middle of the Finnish forest).

# THE WORLD
# IS NOT FLAT

Not all speaking engagements are created equal. Sometimes, you will just deliver the same keynote as last week in some no-name place. Another day, another dollar. These are your horizontal talks. You are doing the same thing in different places, much like Coca-Cola sells the same brown beverage in Kigali and Kalmar. However, if your skills and luck conspire, you will speak at a stellar event that can elevate your stature as a speaker to a new level. You will be very nervous beforehand and forced to make a supreme effort to deliver to your utmost ability. If you succeed, you level up. These vertical events – sending you up into the stratosphere – tend to be superspreaders, meaning that if you make it there, people will book you far and wide. The TED Conference (the big, annual one currently held in Vancouver, Canada) is an example. Gartner Symposiums, annual mega events for IT audiences held over four continents, is another. Horizontal events exploit your brand (but boost your income), whereas vertical events build it.

After a while, the dynamic tends to be self-perpetu-
ating as you earn a reputation for being a sure thing
to have on the big conference stages. This is the holy
grail of the speaking business: the cumulative advantage dubbed The Matthew Effect ("For whosoever
hath shall be given, for whosoever hath not, from him
shall be taken away.").

# CONCLUSION: A SIMPLE RECIPE FOR SUCCESS

It is in the nature of advice on complex topics like health, wealth or happiness that they should be somewhat difficult to grasp. "Avoid things that make you unhappy" just does not cut it as a surefire way to find happiness. That is why you will most certainly reject the following simple advice for success as a speaker: do more of what works, do not seek variety.

Travelling around the world is adventurous and will impress others but it will not necessarily make you a better speaker. A lot of it will be wasted time and carbon dioxide emissions. In the exploratory phase of your career, you may have to stray off the beaten track but once you have proven yourself as an income-generating, pro-level speaker, you are better off finding a comfortable balance between income-boosting and brand-building events. Stand-up comedians have a saying: "You *make* money during the day. You *collect* it at night." This is a semantic distinction between gathering useful, comedic material when you are offstage and then reaping the rewards when you make people laugh hysterically at the comedy club.

Similarly, not all speaking engagements are created equal. Even if – and especially when – they pay a similar amount.

**DO!** Prioritize Strategic Locations: Choose speaking engagements in prestigious locations and major business hubs. These venues are more likely to embrace your message, invite you back and lead to additional high-paying opportunities.

 **DON'T!** Chase Money Blindly: Avoid accepting engagements solely based on the fee without considering the location and potential impact on your reputation. Not all well-paid gigs are worth your time and effort.

 **DO!** Seek Referrals and Repeat Business: Focus on delivering exceptional presentations in locations that can lead to further engagements. A memorable performance in a prime location will often result in more lucrative opportunities.

**DON'T!**   Overlook the Importance of Venue: Don't ignore the significance of where you are speaking. A great performance in a top-tier city can elevate your stature, while a similar performance in a less prestigious location might go unnoticed.

 **DO!**   Balance Income with Brand Building: Find a balance between engagements that boost your income and those that enhance your brand. Aim to secure a mix of both to sustain long-term success.

 **DON'T!**   Neglect Your Personal Life: Don't sacrifice your personal relationships and peace of mind for the sake of constant travel and income. Consider the toll on your well-being and strive for a sustainable schedule.

**DO!** Select High-Impact Events: Identify and pursue events that can serve as vertical launches for your career, such as prestigious conferences and symposiums. These can significantly raise your profile and lead to widespread recognition.

 **DON'T!** Be a Jack of All Trades: Avoid spreading yourself too thin by accepting every opportunity. Focus on engagements that align with your goals and can provide meaningful returns in terms of reputation and future bookings.

**DO!**     Evaluate Each Opportunity: Assess each speaking engagement not just by its fee but by its potential to enhance your reputation, provide valuable referrals and offer a worthwhile experience.

 Compromise on Quality: Never compromise the quality of your presentations. Ensure every performance, regardless of location, is delivered with excellence to maintain your reputation and credibility.

THE FINAL
COMMANDMENT

# THOU SHALT
# SHOW UP

*"Ninety per cent of success in life is just showing up" is a quote that has been attributed to various celebrities throughout the years. When you're toiling away to build a career, it makes no sense. Once you have arrived, you understand it perfectly. With so many things, opportunities and distractions poking away at your limited time and attention, it becomes truly hard to show up. You cancel, call in sick, wait for something – somebody – better. You forget that the foundation you are standing on was built on long years of hard work ... and a generous dose of luck, so you start gambling, chipping away at your fortune. When everyone around your dinner table is on your payroll, you have truly become an asshole. Back to square one you go. The show in show business is about showing up.*

Nearly all big business conferences in São Paolo occur at the World Trade Center in Cidade Monções, a drab block of office buildings next to a constantly congested road. It was here, on an overcast August day in 2014, that the Aço Steel conference took place, and I was the keynote speaker. I landed this engagement by giving good talks at other steel and commodities conferences in South America and felt confident that I could deliver something stellar onstage. After all, the rest of the program consisted of all-male panels discussing the ins and outs of all things steel and manufacturing. A friend is prone to describe my profession with a hint of sarcasm: "Magnus, you are just a mediocre clown at a very boring children's party."

The conference started late, and by lunch – as expected in Brazilian conferences – we were behind schedule by at least an hour. Fortunately, the moderator felt the vibes in the room and called for a short coffee break before I was due to speak. At least I would not have to face that fiercest of speaker foes: low blood sugar. The short break turned into a longish break as there were conversations to be had, pastries to eat and bathrooms to visit. Finally, it was time for me to shine onstage. The atmosphere was ... strange. I am used to people being skeptical when their event is interrupted – the French even call keynote speeches 'interventions' – but this was different. People were not paying attention. Most people were glued to their phone screens. Some even got up and left the room. As a speaker, it is impossible to capture the attention of an entire room lest you do something truly scandalous, but to lose an entire audience within the first few minutes is rare. Given that my reputation from the other commodities conferences preceded me, I felt confident that I could win back their attention. It turned out to be false hope. More and more people started leaving for the exits and, soon enough, a handful of people were left in the room, and all of them were staring at their phones.

It turned out that just as I had started to speak, a plane carrying the presidential candidate Eduardo Campos had crashed in the southern part of the city. With elections due in a few months, he was considered the great hope – a Barack Obama of sorts – that could put the country on the right track. It was a national tragedy. Something no speaker in the world can – or should – try to compete with.

I remember finishing my speech before the near-empty congress hall and the moderator announcing that the remainder of the conference was cancelled.

The show must indeed go on. But that is sometimes hard, even impossible. This chapter will look at some of the reasons and the pitfalls to avoid.

# WHEN REASONS BECOME EXCUSES

There will come a day in your career as a speaker when everything that has worked against you starts working for you. It is a glorious feeling. Rejection, awkward silence, low pay become high fees, standing ovations and social media feeds proclaiming your genius. That is when a different kind of trouble starts. You can divide it into four phases.

1. **Denial:** Difficult to keep commitments

2. **Bargaining:** Making excuses to avoid keeping commitments because something better is happening elsewhere

3. **Arrogance:** Treating the engagements you commit to unprofessionally

4. **Giving Up:** Not showing up at all

**Denial:** First, you start scrambling to keep your commitments. A finance conference had booked me in Barcelona too late one evening to make the last flight home to Stockholm and a speaking engagement the following morning. I chartered a private jet for €20,000 to make it to both engagements. I showed up. But it erased any profits I stood to make that month ... and quarter. In this phase, you learn to run faster to stay in the same place.

**Bargaining:** In the next phase, you suffer from FOMO – fear of missing out, a nicer word for greed – and say yes to everything, knowing there will be scheduling conflicts. Like an overbooked aircraft, you must make concessions and outright lie. When I got more international, better-paid engagements, travelling to small towns in Sweden for less pay suddenly felt a lot less attractive. I called in sick. I had standby speakers ready to take my place. In short, I stopped showing up.

**Arrogance:** I remember taking a late-night flight to Brussels one January evening. The flight path was through stormy weather, and I had to leave my twins' birthday party at home to make the flight. I felt awful, with the guilt manifesting as a fear of flying. It was nothing a glass of red wine – or six, to be more specific – and a cognac could not cure. Although my memory became hazy, I think I had a drink or two at the bar when I arrived at the hotel. Predictably, I awoke with a massive hangover and breath reeking of alcohol the next morning. What I delivered onstage that day can best be described as crap. A giant, steaming pile of dog crap. The client was never heard from again. What had once been my dream job – inspiring people onstage – had become a nightmare of my own making.

**Giving Up:** I got an invitation to speak in Iran. I accepted and they sent a formal invitation to use for the visa application. When I arrived at the Iranian embassy, the line was too long, so I gave up on the idea and started ghosting them. Let me rephrase this, as blaming the length of the queue is lazy. I had become an arrogant fat cat whose curiosity for new cultures and love for the craft of speaking had waned. I should have politely declined the invitation instead of giving them the wrong expectations.

I was to be a keynote speaker at a digital conference in Trinidad and Tobago. I was to bring my family along. When we missed our flight connection, the client wanted to rebook me on a three-stopover, 20-hour flight path that would make bringing my family along impossible. I told the conference organizers that I would be a no-show. They were, of course, outraged. I should have just declined the initial invitation. Or plan my travel better. Or take better care of my family, so being away from them would not be such a source of guilt and shame.

There comes a time when the showing-up part becomes a challenge in and of itself. You sabotage the career you worked hard to build. The real measure of success comes not with the ignition to liftoff but with the ability to maintain a mile-high altitude ... or attitude.

# LOSING TOUCH

Although the exact pace of physical and cognitive decline varies between individuals, it begins at some point in your mid- to late-40s.

The rapid pace of development in the world around us accelerates the gap between the powers you once possessed and the landscape unfolding before you.

The arrival of the social media platform TikTok in the early 2020s made me feel like I made horseshoes in a time of the automobile.

I had become a craftsman fewer people needed.

It happens to everyone.

Silent film actors were out of work when the 'talkies' came.

Typesetters, which placed metal fonts in racks and added ink to print things, were lost when laser printers and computers entered the scene.

To say nothing of the people who just lost touch. Genius film directors who started making bad movies. Pop stars who aged out of the lucrative youth market. Fashion designers who could no longer feel where the market was heading.

Showing up does not just mean continuing to do your work in the face of adversity. It also means staying curious, adapting to new trends and not being afraid of abandoning your old convictions. It is not an antidote to ageing but an inhibitor that enables you to keep going for another couple of years, even if TikTok videos have thrown a spanner in your work.

# CONCLUSION:
# THE SHOW
# MUST GO ON

Failure is a better teacher than success. This is why this book has been littered with my failures and shortcomings, not my triumphs. As I was writing them down, it dawned on me that they had all happened as I was going through hardship in my private life. The Denmark debacle described in the Fourth Commandment happened when my marriage was falling apart. The travel needed to sustain a speaking career will take its toll on any relationship.

The project management conference in Rome described in the same chapter happened as my father lay dying back in Sweden. Being human is a struggle. We all go through bad things in life, and we all suffer neuroses, anxiety and depression. Yet, the audience does not care. They are there for a day of inspiration or an evening of infotainment. Whatever you are going through at home, do not take it with you up onstage.

Advice that is impossible to live up to, of course.

It is neither possible nor desirable never to have a bad day at the office. Being a speaker is about being relatable more than it is about being perfect.

But longevity in any career is about consistency. It sounds easy, but boredom, arrogance and laziness will get in your way sooner or later.

When you stumble or fall, as you most certainly will, pick yourself up, dust yourself off and keep walking. The memories of clients, audiences and the world is surprisingly short.

Failures are lessons, not prison sentences.

Be kind to yourself.

And to other speakers.

This is not a race or a zero-sum game.

It is a long and perilous journey.

For which thou shalt show up.

**DO!**    Show Up Consistently:
Always honour your commitments
and show up for every
engagement, regardless of
circumstances. Your reputation is
built on reliability and consistency.

 **DON'T!**    Make Excuses:
Avoid making excuses for not
showing up. Whether it's personal
issues or better opportunities,
prioritize the commitments you
have made.

 **DO!**    Stay Humble and Professional:
Maintain humility and
professionalism, even as you gain
success. Remember that your
career is built on years of hard
work and a bit of luck. Respect
every opportunity.

 **DON'T!**    Cancel Without Good Reason:
Don't cancel engagements last
minute without a compelling
reason. It damages your
reputation and can hurt
relationships with clients and
event organizers.

**DO!** Manage Your Schedule Wisely: Plan your travel and engagements carefully to avoid burnout and ensure you can meet all your commitments without sacrificing quality or personal well-being.

 **DON'T!** Overcommit: Avoid saying yes to everything out of greed or fear of missing out. Overcommitting leads to stress, poor performance and potential cancellations.

 **DO!** Adapt to Changing Trends: Stay curious and adaptable. Keep up with new trends and technologies to remain relevant in the ever-evolving speaking industry.

 **DON'T!** Ignore Personal Well-being: Don't neglect your mental and physical health. Balance your professional commitments with personal time to maintain long-term success.

**DO!**  Learn from Failures:
Use your failures as learning
experiences. They are valuable
for personal and professional
growth. Share these lessons to
help others and build a more
relatable persona.

 Let Success Make You Complacent:
Avoid becoming complacent
or arrogant due to success.
Always strive for improvement
and stay grounded.

 **DO!**  Be Relatable:
Show your human side and
connect with your audience
on a personal level. Authenticity
and relatability are more
important than perfection.

 Take Personal Struggles Onstage:
While it's important to be human,
try not to let personal issues
affect your performance. The
audience is there for inspiration
and entertainment.

OUTRO

# THE LONG FADE

It was the largest ballroom I had ever seen. As far as the eye could see, there were rows upon rows of chairs. In just a few hours, thousands of people would fill the room. They had not come to see me. I was merely a support act. They were there for Alexey Gordeev, Russia's Minister of Agriculture at the time. The event was a part of Agrivision, the biggest agricultural conference in Russia, and among the biggest in the world in 2008. It was an era of globalization and collaboration. In Sweden, we had all been taught that Russia was no longer the evil empire of Soviet times but am emerging economy, a sleeping giant about to wake up and, together with Brazil, India and China, part of the much-hyped BRICs countries[5] that were to overtake us all in terms of economic growth, innovation and business momentum. What an exciting time to be alive and what a privilege to speak in Moscow.

The very first speaker of the day was a former Soviet general wearing a military uniform with stars and medals on it. His presence puzzled me. Why would Russia want a Soviet general onstage? Wouldn't that be like Germans putting a nazi onstage?

He spoke in a manner you did not see in a democracy. He waved his arms and shouted strong statements across the room. I wore headphones to hear the translation. "We were once the biggest agricultural manufacturer in the world," the translator said, staccato style. "Then we had the 90s crisis ... but now, dear guests, we will rise again!"

It dawned on me that the narrative we had been given in the West was false.

The Soviet Union collapsed, but the Russian spirit lived on. What we thought was a new dawn in the 1990s was, for them, a time of crisis and humiliation.

Vladimir Putin had put them back on track to become a superpower.

The audience clapped enthusiastically. The general was a hero and a reminder of all the great things that once were and would be again.

Before I was due to speak, the moderator made an announcement.

I had taken my headphones off, so I could not understand what was said, but the result was dramatic. A murmur rose from the crowd, and the vast majority got up and left the room.

I heard my name being called and got up to speak for the decimated crowd.

---

5   An intergovernmental organization originally comprising Brazil, Russia, India, China and, later on, South Africa, Iran, Egypt, Ethiopia and the United Arab Emirates.

It turned out that Minister Gordeev had been asked to accompany President Putin at the last minute on an official visit to Brazil. There would be no chance to hobnob with the elite, so what was the point of staying to watch some unknown Swede with no political clout in Russia, the audience seemed to think.

My engagement in Russia was good business – the pay was exorbitant – but it was a very bad speech.

Furthermore, it points to an often-overlooked aspect of business: ethics.

I had no way of knowing that Russian tanks would a few years later roll into Krim and, a decade after that, into Ukraine, slaughtering civilians. But I was naive about the world in 2008. I had a dream of becoming a speaker who could make a living by travelling the world and inspiring people. The dream came true.

The nightmare, too.

Somebody once said, show me a great fortune, and I will show you a great crime.

With business overlooking ethics, this statement makes perfect sense. As a speaker, you rarely stop to think about whether it is right to sound like you know things, to travel wherever and get paid by whomever. You may hide behind the fact that what you are doing is merely infotainment, as opposed to, say, selling weapons or cigarettes. But the words you exhale and the planes you travel on emit carbon dioxide. The work I did in Russia has haunted me. Not because Russian people are inherently evil. On the contrary, many of the people I met on my trips there have expressed strong anti-war opinions in my correspondence with them since the Ukrainian invasion. What has haunted me was that I never spoke up, forewarned or expressed my distaste. It was not my role. I was paid to entertain and inspire. Speaking my mind would have been bad business.

But it would have been brave.

It would have been right.

# BEING WRONG

There are two types of lying. The first is to share an untruth, usually about yourself to get some kind of advantage or attention. Even a white lie is still a lie. The second kind is not to correct untruths shared about you by other people. If somebody says you are a doctor when you are a nurse, not correcting them constitutes a type-two lie.

As a speaker, I have committed many type-two lies, especially when others proclaim that I can foresee or predict the future.

This is why my presentation for hotel managers in London in February 2020 is so damning. My presentation was well liked, but given the outbreak of the COVID pandemic a month later, its half-life was very short.

I spent years raving about social media's potential to bring world peace through greater interconnection. The Cambridge Analytica scandal, in which Facebook was hijacked for political purposes, proved me wrong.

These things are not evil. They were well intentioned but wrong.

Yet the outcome trumps the intentions, so the end result became somebody who was presented as having the gift of prophecy and telling lies onstage.

I did good business as a speaker, but I didn't always do good.

This is the crack in the business lens. It is blind to things that cannot be calculated in dollars and cents. It is blind to things that are invisible yet vital for humanity.

Business can tell you how to make money. But not why.

And it does not show you a path to happiness.

Capitalism's biggest trick is that it abolished the concept of enough. You can always strive for more.

Although the money I've earned has provided for my family – a house, school, vacations and a car – it did not bring peace of mind, lasting happiness or even a finite sense of accomplishment.

This is why you need to bring other perspectives to the art of speaking, not just an ability to make money. We often think of careers along an axis with money on one side and time on the other. You tend to lose the other if you tilt toward one side on this axis. Investment bankers are rich but work all the time, while part-time musicians are broke. There is, however, another dimension on this scale: freedom. The money-rich and time-poor banker will not be free to challenge his (it is most often he, statistically speaking) employer or dream up whatever projects he likes. The broke musician may be unfree to pursue whatever endeavours they like since money is too tight to mention. Freedom – intellectual, spiritual or practical – is more valuable than money and time. You learn that after you have explored the one-dimensional money/time axis.

Life is greater than business. While going to Bali or Belgium may very well be bad business decisions for a speaker, they can nourish the soul and open new perspectives.

# THE FUTURE IS UNWRITTEN

Experience is what middle-aged men call their mistakes. Doing business is not a precise science but a mix of the rational and irrational. My advice in this book is blind to my own shadow. It may have been all luck. I am a tall white male born in a prosperous part of the world to middle-class parents. I won the lucky sperm lottery. The rise of my speaking career coincided with zero interest rates, an abundance of cheap capital and high insecurity about the future.

However, understanding why something has succeeded historically is of lesser significance in business than understanding that there are an infinite number of ways to be successful. The optimistic perspective is to believe that most of them have not happened yet. The best speakers have not been born, and the best speeches have not been given. The coolest gadgets and most profitable industries still hide the fog of tomorrow.

The large language models (LLMs) powering the current incarnation of artificial intelligence have enabled iterations at hyper-speed to play around with words, ideas and images. The toolbox with which speakers can amplify their message has both deepened and widened.

The blend of digital and physical realms – as seen in Metaverse creations like the game Fortnite or the ABBA show in London and in the all-encompassing screen of The Sphere in Las Vegas – will enable speeches to be delivered in brand new ways, just like PowerPoint and digital projectors once did.

Speakers are increasingly being used as micro-task consultants, not just entertaining but delivering answers and suggestions to narrow tasks, delivered in less than an hour and crafted to be more persuasive and inspirational than your standard management consultants.

The traditional view of a physical workplace and an eight-hour workweek is being challenged by work-from-home schemes, hybrid workplaces and massive online collaboration platforms.

This is merely scratching the surface of what will become of an industry built on the human larynx's power to convey ideas. Besides, people will always need consoling fables about the human condition, whether cloaked as futurology or self-help.

# BECOMING

Once upon a time, we saw human beings as fixed and stagnant. You were either born a pauper or a princess. Nowadays, we see human beings as being changeable and fluid. We can change our gender, sexuality, appearance and our minds. This is why the most important part of this book's subtitle is not "success" or "business" but "becoming."

Success is not an entitlement. Everybody's free to start or open things whenever they want, but nobody controls when it comes to closing down or finishing. I've tried leaving the speaker business many times. When the pandemic struck in 2020, I – like many others – assumed that live events and conferences were condemned to the past and enrolled in the police academy.

Having been a one-man show for nearly two decades, I was eager to join a uniformed, deindividualized entity like the police force. I wanted to stamp out my ego completely.

It was not to be.

Every time I try to leave, the speaking world pulls me back in, to quote that mafia movie.

And though I have sworn about the loneliness of business travel and the shame you feel when your speeches do not go well, there are magical moments when delivering a keynote speech is the most meaningful thing in the world.

Not least when it happens in places that need hope.

I remember speaking in Karachi in 2012 when Al Qaeda was busy murdering polio vaccination workers in the city. It is a chaotic country, politically a failed state, yet full of people trying to lead normal lives, dreaming big about the future.

I'm continually surprised by how accommodating and versatile the speaking industry is. It has room for anyone or anything. Diversity is an issue in other industries but in the speaking world, it is the raison d'être. A transgender Native American mixing anthropological research with EDM music might have a hard time getting a job in an investment bank but would easily give talks at 30k a pop in no time.

I have trained for the speaking profession my whole life. There's nothing I'd rather do in life.

At the age of ten, I dreamed of being a rock star. I would set up a pretend stage in the garden and hum songs in my head, using a badminton racket as a guitar.

The grass and bushes around me were the audience.

They looked happy.

In *The Age of Reason*, Jean-Paul Sartre wrote that a life is formed from the future. Everybody, everywhere, wants something. To happen, to come true, to change. When these dreams of tomorrow start to fade, your life will begin to run out.

Don't be afraid of dreaming.

Don't shy away from the s-word.

Become who you were meant to be.

Bite into something before your teeth are gone.

I look forward to meeting you on the speaking circuit very soon.

# BOOK BLURB

Ever wondered how to transform your love for speaking into a lucrative profession? In *The Business of Speaking*, Magnus Lindkvist, a globally acclaimed trendspotter and futurologist, unpacks the journey from free gigs to high-paying engagements. With humour and hard-won wisdom, Lindkvist reveals his ten commandments for speaking success, offering a blend of practical tips and personal anecdotes. This book is your guide to crafting compelling talks, handling criticism and making a living by captivating audiences around the world.

Through real-life stories and insightful advice, Magnus takes you behind the scenes of the speaking industry, sharing his personal journey from obscurity to fame. He emphasizes the importance of building a strong, consistent speaking product, understanding the nuances of different audiences, and mastering the art of continuous improvement. Whether you are an aspiring speaker or a seasoned professional looking to elevate your career, this book provides a comprehensive road map to becoming a successful speaker.

*The Business of Speaking* goes beyond mere techniques, delving into the mindset and strategies needed to thrive in this competitive field. Learn how to embrace failures, turn criticism into growth opportunities, and develop a speech that resonates with diverse audiences. Magnus Lindkvist's insights will inspire you to push boundaries and achieve greatness in the world of public speaking.

# ABOUT
# THE AUTHOR

**Magnus Lindkvist** is a visionary futurologist and trendspotter, renowned for his subversively humorous and insightful keynotes. With a master's in business and economics from the Stockholm School of Economics and a film production degree from UCLA, Magnus combines academic rigour with Hollywood storytelling. Over nearly three decades, he has enthralled audiences globally, sharing profound insights into creativity, innovation and future trends.

Lindkvist's unique approach has made him a sought-after speaker at conferences, corporations and institutions worldwide. He is the author of several thought-provoking books on future thinking and trendspotting, and his dynamic presentations have inspired countless individuals and organizations to embrace the future with curiosity and imagination.

A native of Sweden, Magnus is often described as one of the country's greatest exports, next to ABBA and meatballs. He brings a unique blend of Scandinavian pragmatism and visionary thinking to his work, making complex ideas accessible and engaging. When he's not travelling the world for speaking engagements, Magnus enjoys delving into new ideas, exploring different cultures and spending time with his family.

For more on Magnus Lindkvist and his work, visit magnuslindkvist.com.